The Christian Mind

The Christian Mind

Escaping Futility

Banner Mini-Guides
The Christian Mind

William Edgar

THE BANNER OF TRUTH TRUST

THE BANNER OF TRUTH TRUST

Head Office	*North America Office*
3 Murrayfield Road	PO Box 621
Edinburgh, EH12 6EL	Carlisle, PA 17013
UK	USA

banneroftruth.org

© The Banner of Truth Trust, 2018
First published 2018
Revised edition 2020

ISBN
Print: 978 1 84871 815 9
EPUB: 978 1 84871 816 6
Kindle: 978 1 84871 817 3

*

Typeset in 10/14 pt Minion Pro
at the Banner of Truth Trust, Edinburgh

Printed in the USA by
Versa Press, Inc.,
East Peoria, IL

To

SCOTT AND PEGGY OLIPHINT

Best travelling companions

Contents

Preface

A book of this size cannot possibly treat the great subject of 'the Christian Mind' in much detail. It is a 'mini-guide', one of a series that will introduce the reader to some of the major themes and issues related to the Christian faith. Each one will provide an outline of the Bible's teaching on a particular subject. They will open up a key verse or portion of Scripture for study, while not neglecting other passages related to the theme under consideration. The goal is to whet your appetite and to encourage you to explore the subject in more detail: hence the suggestions for further reading which appear after the final chapter. However, the mini-guide will provide enough information to enlarge your understanding of the theme.

All the mini-guides have been arranged in a thirteen-chapter format so that they will seamlessly fit into the teaching quarters of the church year and be useful for Sunday School lessons or Bible class studies.

By way of acknowledgement I wish to express my deepest gratitude to the excellent editors at the Banner of Truth Trust. I especially want to thank my dear friend Mark Johnston for kindly including me in this series of mini-guides, and for his steady guidance throughout. My thanks also extend to Westminster Theological Seminary for their generous sabbatical policy which provided the time and resources to complete this book. Lastly, but not least, I wish to thank my precious wife, Barbara, for her patient companionship through this and many other projects.

BILL EDGAR
October 2017

Introduction

For some a series on the Christian mind might seem so obvious as not to be necessary. Of course one's faith ought to be thought through, otherwise we will remain spiritual children, 'tossed to and fro by the waves and carried about by every wind of doctrine' (Eph. 4:14). Is it not precisely because of such threats that we need to reinforce our commitment to clear thinking? Is not one of the curses of our day the very absence of sound discernment, a curse that has penetrated the church itself?

Yet we don't need a plea for just *any* thinking. Another blight of our time is the opposite of mindlessness. It is trusting too much in the unaided human capacity to reason things through. In our scientific age we often are presented with claims from studies, or experiments, or experts that 'prove' this or that theory.

In this book, and the series that follows, we wish to strike a balance between the proper use of our minds and the need to depend on the grace of God at every point. God uses our minds in our communion with him. As we will try to show, the use of the mind is not opposed to faith but is its fruit. And the human effort required to develop a good mind does not contradict the grace of God but rather grows out of it.

In this quest we could do far worse than be guided by one of the great theologians of the Christian church, John Owen (1616–83). In his book, *The Grace and Duty of Being Spiritually Minded*, he explains that to be spiritual is to be full of eternal blessedness.[1] Taking his starting point from Romans 8:6, he draws a contrast throughout the book between the way of death and the way of life. For Owen, enormous human effort and the grace of God are not at odds with each other, but entail one another. Here is how he puts it:

> Nothing can be so ruinous to our profession, as once to suppose it is an easy matter, a thing of course, to maintain our peace with God. God forbid that our utmost diligence, and continued endeavours to thrive in every grace, should not be required thereto. The whole beauty and glory of our religion depends hereon. To be spiritually minded is life and peace.[2]

As you read through these pages we hope you will be enriched, and that you will be encouraged to use your mind with reverence and gratitude.

[1] John Owen, *The Grace and Duty of Being Spiritually Minded, Declared and Practically Improved* (New York: Robert Carter, 1848).

[2] Owen, *Grace and Duty of Being Spiritually Minded*, pp. 326-27.

1

Are Christians Mindless?

After making this complaint about the lack of Christian thinking today, one will sometimes meet with the astonishing reply that there is no longer any need for Christian thinking.

—Harry Blamires[1]

We hear it in a thousand ways from a thousand sources: *Faith is irrational.* Mark Twain, the sceptical American author of novels such as *Tom Sawyer* and *Huckleberry Finn,* once quipped, '[Faith is] believing what you know ain't so.'[2] Predictably, the various 'new atheists' tell us that there is a fundamental incompatibility between religious belief and evidence-based science. Despite repeated refutations by such very different critics as Jonathan Sacks, Rowan Williams, and John Lennox, Richard Dawkins persists in declaring that, 'Because the

[1] Harry Blamires (1916–2017) was an Anglican theologian, literary critic, and novelist.
[2] Mark Twain, *Following the Equator: A Journey around the World* (New York: Dover Publications, 1989), p. 132.

moderates are so nice we all are brought up with the idea that there is something good about religious faith … that there is something good about bringing children up to have a faith … Which means to believe something without evidence and without the need for justifying it.'[1] Faith for him, and for many others, by definition requires no rational grounds. And he adds that this view is actually dangerous. It's all masked behind being nice. Nice people don't probe into other people's faith. And because they don't, it means terrorists are immune to any criticisms of their views.

Mysticism

This understanding, that faith is not rational, is not only propounded by unbelievers, who mean it as a criticism. It can often be found defended by believers, who mean it as a good thing. It is not uncommon to hear Christian people claim, 'I can get this far by my reason, but then I must let go thinking about it and go on by faith.' Some will appeal to Scriptures such as Ephesians 3:19, where the apostle Paul prays that his readers will be able 'to know the love of Christ that surpasses knowledge.' The argument goes, knowledge can bring us to a certain place, but then faith must take over, because knowledge cannot get us to the deepest experience of the love of Christ, or, as the rest of the verse says it, to 'the fullness of God.' One might call such a view mysticism. Mysticism comes in many guises. What most strands have

[1] Cited by Melanie McDonagh, 'Richard Dawkins Doesn't Get it: Religion is Rational,' *Spectator*, [https://blogs.spectator.co.uk/2014/08/richard-dawkins-doesnt-get-it-religion-is-rational/#]

in common is the idea that in order to have communion with God at the highest level we must abandon our reason and yield to God's overwhelming presence. Often, mystics believe we must abolish the self and become channels of a spiritual force beyond ourselves.

As in all such notions, there is a part truth in this view. There are things about God far too deep for our comprehension. Often people in the Bible are admonished for thinking they could put God in a box. Remember poor Job, who was reprimanded for darkening counsel 'by words without knowledge' (Job 38:2). Or think of the people of Israel whom the prophet had to reprove: 'For my thoughts are not your thoughts, neither are your ways my ways, declares the LORD. For as the heavens are higher than the earth, so are my ways higher than your ways and my thoughts than your thoughts' (Isa. 55:8, 9). Indeed, one might say that there is nothing about God's ways, nor his nature, that is not in some ways beyond our comprehension.

But that is not at all the same as saying, 'thus far by knowledge, and then onward by faith.' Why would faith be able to grasp what our knowledge cannot? It is worth asking, in Ephesians 3, what kind of knowledge the apostle is talking about that is being surpassed? It cannot be all knowledge. He had just finished expressing the hope that by faith his readers would *comprehend* with all the saints, 'what is the breadth and length and height and depth.' He wants them to *know* the love of Christ that surpasses knowledge. Surely, then, the knowledge that can be surpassed is ordinary human knowledge. Such knowledge is good in itself.

3

There is great wisdom available in the world, and much of it has produced great achievements. But there is still more: there is a knowledge that gives strength, a knowledge that leads to the love of Christ, which is not available through ordinary human means. Such knowledge is not irrational. It requires faith to achieve, but this faith does not invalidate this great fourfold wisdom of God, rather it leads us to it. God wants us to have knowledge, but the kind that is beyond mere humanly wrought knowledge.

Certainly there can be bad arguments, ones that hinder coming to faith. To the Corinthians the apostle Paul cites two such false arguments, criteria raised by those who object to the Christian message. He groups them together as the wisdom of the world, and explains why they stand in the way (2 Cor. 1:18-25). The first is what he calls a 'stumbling block to the Jews.' The majority of God's ancient people could not accept that their messiah had to perish on a Roman gibbet. The cross was an instrument of shame and death. It was devised for criminals, and many Jews considered it quite absurd that the Son of God should be its victim. The second he names 'folly to the Gentiles.' The non-Jews, often lumped together as 'the Greeks,' had a different problem with the cross. It appeared incompatible with the lofty rationalist philosophies believed by the ancient world. It seemed petty, irrelevant. That the essence of truth was found, not in Greek philosophy, but in God's humiliation, was not a dignified idea. It was not worthy of great thinking. Incidentally many in our own time share such a view.

Nevertheless, the apostle tells his readers that 'Jesus and him crucified' is not only the absolute truth, but a worldview that explodes these and every human objection (1 Cor. 2:2). Using considerable rhetorical skill, Paul tells them this foolishness according to the world is the very key that unlocks all of life's mysteries. It is a wisdom which none of the rulers of the world can understand, because they lack the humility to receive it. Yet by the Spirit of God this divine wisdom may be understood by his people (1 Cor. 2:10-13). So, not only is the truth of the gospel of a different order from the way of the world, but the very manner by which it is accessed is different.

The important point for us here is that even though this truth and its access are unique, they are not irrational. Paul says the natural person does not accept the things of the Spirit of God, not because they are beyond reason, but because they do not originate in a proud human philosophy (1 Cor. 2:14-16). Faith in the gospel is not an irrational leap, but a posture of humility. The author of Hebrews agrees. Just because we cannot see all of it, does not mean it is untrue. The Christian mind understands this.

Mindless Ways

In an insightful little book published in 1972 English evangelical leader John Stott describes three types of anti-intellectuals within the Christian church.[1] Each of them regards theology with distaste and distrust. The first

---

[1] John R. W. Stott, *Your Mind Matters: The Place of the Mind in the Christian Life* (Leicester: Inter-Varsity Press, 1972), chapter 1.

type of anti-intellectual person is attracted to ritual and liturgy. Stott is careful to distinguish between proper ritual and ritualism, where the performance of ritual becomes an end in itself, a meaningless substitute for intelligent worship. The second type of anti-intellectual person he identifies with radical Christianity, in which there is a concentration of energy on social and political action to the neglect of all else. Stott is critical of the ecumenical movement which seeks to bring churches and Christians together for the way it has emphasized social action at the expense of truth. Concern for the poor, for race issues, and the like are of course urgent Christian priorities. But Stott finds fault with such contemporary movements for giving them the monopoly of our commitments. The ecumenical movement despairs over ever reaching doctrinal agreement, and therefore takes refuge in activism. One of the slogans of the ecumenical movement was 'doctrine divides, service unites.' The third type of anti-intellectual person within the church Stott identifies with the excesses of the Pentecostal movement. While Stott wrote a number of critical pieces on charismatic 'second blessing' theology, his simple point here is that many who hold to that teaching are so committed to experience that they avoid becoming involved in anything else. In effect they put subjective experience above God's revealed truth.

Stott goes on to argue that these three types are symptoms of the same malady of anti-intellectualism. 'They are escape routes by which to avoid our God-given responsibility to use our minds Christianly.'[1] Today we continue to see these and other similar trends in the church. But an important qualifier must be brought to bear. The answer to anti-intellectualism must not be intellectualism. There is a kind of cold, overly rational thinking in some parts of the church, as well as in theological seminaries, which is somehow obsessed with minutiae at the expense of the glorious whole. Our Lord is particularly severe against the established religion of his day for that kind of thinking:

> Woe to you, scribes and Pharisees, hypocrites! For you tithe mint and dill and cumin and have neglected the weightier matters of the law, justice and mercy and faithfulness. These you ought to have done, without neglecting the others. You blind guides, straining out a gnat and swallowing a camel! (Matt. 23:23, 24)

While there is a crucial place for theological precision and confessional exactness, when the concern for precise formulation of doctrine begins to crowd out the larger concerns, a malady has crept in which is often difficult to cure.

It is important for us not to forget the purpose of doctrine. The apostle Paul tells his young child in the faith Timothy to steer people away from 'myths and endless genealogies, which promote speculations rather than the stewardship from God that is by faith' (1 Tim. 1:4; see also Titus 3:9). The preoccupation with secondary matters can be strangely seductive to some. Why this fixation on genealogies? We mustn't think people were looking up their

---

[1] Stott, *Your Mind Matters*, p. 17.

7

ancestry to find out if they were related to some famous figure from the past as we might do today. Most likely the Jewish Christians were clinging to their status, and anxious to hold on to their ancestry. This was true particularly after King Herod destroyed the public registers, no doubt out of jealousy against the noble origins of the Jews. The heresy of Gnosticism, which was popular in the Greek-speaking world of the first and second centuries AD, taught that you could get closer to God if you could prove your authentic origins, and also practise certain Old Testament rituals. This led those who followed Gnostic teachings to intellectualism.

Christian faith is not intellectualist, but it does depend on the intellect. So what are the origins of 'mindless Christianity'?

2

The Larger Setting for Mindlessness

If we are to be heard by a generation that prizes safety above free speech, we must work hard at grasping the immensity of our task and realize that for all sorts of reasons ... there is more tribal and less common ground than ever.

—Richard Cunningham[1]

Prejudice against thinking does not come in a vacuum. Years ago a book critical of America became a surprising best-seller throughout the English-speaking world. Alan Bloom's *The Closing of the American Mind* (1987) could be found on every coffee table, though it is not certain how many people actually read it.[2] The title resonated with a good many. It was a critique of relativism, the idea that

---

[1] Richard Cunningham is Director of Universities and Colleges Christian Fellowship (UCCF). Previously he was Executive Director of the Areopagus Trust, developing initiatives to confront secular thought in universities across Britain and Europe.

[2] Alan Bloom, *The Closing of the American Mind* (New York: Simon & Schuster, 1987).

every point of view is equally valid. The subtitle says, *How Higher Education Has Failed Democracy and Impoverished the Souls of Today's Students*. Quite an indictment! When readers delved more deeply into the book they discovered that Bloom's hero is the French Enlightenment utopian philosopher Jean-Jacques Rousseau (1712–78). He was no real friend of the Christian faith, but his rather blind trust in unaided reason drew many, including Christians, to respect him. Bloom argues that we've left off being reasonable people. He adds that if only we could return to the great books, particularly the Western canon, we could salvage the situation.

Knowledge or Opinion

The great problem of our time, says Bloom, is relativism. At the university this means nothing is absolute, no one philosophy is true. We must allow all points of view, and never impose our own on others. He notes the irony, one many have underscored, that the call to an open mind by relativists ends in an oppressive absolutism: from listening to other points of view to respecting them, to regarding them all as equally valid, and then to intolerance of anyone who cannot agree with relativist doctrine. Thus, one must always ask the relativist: *relative to what?*

Relativism is often first cousin to pragmatism. One of today's most thoughtful social critics is Roger Scruton. He agrees with Alan Bloom and adds that in many modern universities the pursuit of pragmatics has replaced the pursuit of truth.[1] Courses preparing students for various skills have replaced courses in the grand themes of literature, which are deemed elitist. Today, one may study business administration, hotel management, international relations, all meant to prepare the student for life, yet none of them providing any moral compass. Scruton's answer for all this is to get back to the notion of truth, fostered in the great books. Scruton rather movingly tells of a visit he made to an underground seminar in Prague. The students were longing to find an alternative to the lies they had been told under communism. They had discovered Plato, the ancient Greek philosopher (*c.* 428–348 BC), and praised his famous distinction between opinion and knowledge. Opinion is the enemy of knowledge, and a disease which infects the brain by making it incapable of distinguishing between true and false ideas. The students in the seminar were willing to pay a high price for real knowledge. They were willing to oppose communist opinion, and this could cost them harassment, arrest, deprivation and a life on the margins.[2]

The bold claim of the Enlightenment was that through human reason alone, progress could be made toward a happier, freer, improved way of life. Though there were very different expressions of Enlightenment philosophy in the seventeenth and eighteenth centuries, it is fair to

---

[1] Roger Scruton, 'The End of the University', *First Things*, #252, April, 2015, pp. 25-30.

[2] Scruton, 'The End of the University', p. 29. Plato's term 'opinion' does not quite coincide with ours. He did not have in mind honestly held opinions, but prejudice.

summarize them with two themes. German philosopher Immanuel Kant (1724–1804) expressed them best in his essay, *What Is Enlightenment?* (1784). He defines the heart of the matter as the release of humanity from its self-incurred immaturity: 'immaturity is the inability to use one's own understanding without the guidance of another.'[1] Accordingly, for the Enlightenment thinker, this confidence to rely on our own intellect is paired with a suspicion of, or even a hostility toward, other types of authority, particularly stemming from traditional religion.

As it happened, to make a long story short, the Enlightenment ended up cutting off the branch it sat on. The trajectory of trusting in reason and throwing off the shackles of tradition was never ending. New forms of authority which claimed to be reasonable emerged with a vice-grip on any others who got in the way. Of course, reason can do many things, but it cannot provide an adequate basis for meaning, fulfilment, human flourishing. Instead, it desperately looks for them in limited places, places incapable of bearing the weight of life's complexities. Eventually many thinkers stopped claiming the Enlightenment's promise and admitted the only thing left was raw power.

The evangelical theologian and author David Wells (1939–) finds this same dilemma present within the church. He shows how the shallow theologies of our day are vainly attempting to replace the older way, the way of a Christian

---

[1] *Kant: Political Writings*, ed. H. S. Reiss, tr. H. B. Nisbet, 2nd, enlarged edition (Cambridge: Cambridge University Press, 1991), p. 54.

mind. In his brilliant series, beginning with *No Place for Truth*, he highlights two of these shallow views which have taken the place of the robust theology of yesterday: psychology and management.[1] The psychologist cares far more about shoring-up the self than looking for truth. The manager wants to fix things, and run the church like a business, rather than subject it to the spiritual principles of the gospel.[2] What was at first proclaimed as a liberation from the abstractions of theology and the authoritarian hierarchy of the church, now becomes its own oppression. The concentration on the self has often become an imprisonment rather than a proper focus on personhood. Consider, for example, how instead of 'You are wrong,' we are more likely to hear, 'You are insensitive.' Instead of telling someone, 'This is not true,' we are likely to tell them, 'I find what you say offensive.'

Most of us have no desire to be either insensitive or offensive, and yet when we have strong convictions, we would rather someone give objective reasons why we might be right or wrong, not a diagnosis that we have a personal problem, or that we don't fit in. To put it in Plato's terms,

---

[1] David F. Wells, *No Place for Truth: Or Whatever Happened to Evangelical Theology?* (Grand Rapids: Eerdmans, 1993). Others in the series include, *God in the Wasteland* (1994), *Losing Our Virtue* (1998), *Above all Earthly Powers* (2005), and *The Courage to Be Protestant* (2008). Wells is indebted to Robert Bellah's evaluation of the West. In his *Habits of the Heart: Individualism and Commitment in American Life* (Berkeley & Los Angeles, CA: University of California Press, 1985), Bellah names two types of preferred leaders for today, the psychologist and the manager.

[2] Wells, *No Place for Truth*, p. 114.

we would rather hear that we have transgressed the tenets of knowledge than that we have unacceptable opinions.

Identity Politics

Many opinions, in Plato's sense, begin with a laudable concern, based on knowledge. The fight against slavery, culminating in its abolition, peacefully in Great Britain, and violently in North America, was finally accomplished because of the knowledge of such things as biblical norms of justice, a respect for God's image-bearers regardless of colour, and the sins of greed and corruption. The successes of democracy over tyranny were often the result of a better understanding of the human capacity for good and for evil.

But these legitimate appeals to knowledge, when they do not have an adequate basis, soon become uncontrolled ideologies. How may we preserve an adequate philosophical basis for a sound knowledge that will not devolve into ideology? Mathematician and philosopher Alfred North Whitehead (1861–1947) thought Western philosophy was ultimately more powerful than charismatic leaders:

> The great conquerors, from Alexander to Caesar, and from Caesar to Napoleon, influenced profoundly the lives of subsequent generations. But the total effect of this influence shrinks to insignificance if compared to the entire transformation of human habits and human mentality by the long line of men of thought from Thales to the present day, men individually powerless, but ultimately the rulers of the world.[1]

[1] Quoted in Donald W. Treadgold, *The West in China: Religious and*

This is an important point to remember. However much we may be beset with ideologies, they come and go. They will eventually yield to universal ideals. But what Whitehead leaves out is *which* human habits, *what* human mentality can really rule the world? He implies that Western philosophy will do the job. We will argue that only a truly Christian mind can achieve such a beneficial and just rule.

The disturbing thing is that what is known as 'identity thinking' has crept into the Christian church. Identity theologies are fragmenting many seminaries, denominations, and Christian universities. Entire theologies have grown out of a sense of injustice against particular identity groups. For example, black theology, liberation theology, womanist theology, are now legitimate disciplines within the different parts of the church. Once again, there was a need for a redress. Mainstream theology was insufficiently aware of race issues, power groups, and gender oppression. But too often the baby is thrown out with the bath water. The focus on race can obscure the biblical appeal for counting others better (Phil. 2:3). The focus on government oppression can obscure the need for proclaiming the gospel in every circumstance, including persecution (Acts 4:19, 20). The focus on gender can obscure the need for recognizing the unity within the diversity between the sexes (1 Cor. 11:8, 9).

Secular Thought in Modern Times, Vol. I, Russia, 1472-1917 (Cambridge: Cambridge University Press, 1973), p. xxx.

The point here is that this concentration on identity takes a valid concern and magnifies it at the expense of the whole. It diverts the call to strive for knowledge. Ironically, it becomes incapable of bringing forth the very justice it so longs to enact. As one thoughtful author puts it, identity theology produces 'a false justice, because it lacks the divine righteousness that gives meaning to all lesser forms of justice. Call it retribution theology, a form of tribalism at its worst.'[1]

In the Name of Truth

If we want to let go of the opinions of narrow identity politics and identity theology, and replace them by knowledge, a caution is required. There is knowledge and there is knowledge. Plato's philosophy represents a milestone in Western thought, but it is not fundamentally biblical. That may come as a surprise to those who assume the ancient Greeks were, if not essentially compatible with the scriptural outlook, at least a stepping stone toward biblical revelation. The early church Fathers recognized the wisdom of the Greeks, but eventually the church began to realize there was a central difference between the Greek view of truth and that of the Bible.

To put it simply, according to the ancient Greeks truth is a set of timeless abstractions. Connected with beauty and goodness, for Plato truth is in the ultimate forms. These are basically ideas, the objective blueprints of perfection.

[1] Case Thorpe, 'A Seminary Snubs a Presbyterian Pastor,' in *Wall Street Journal*, March 23, 2017.

The forms are rarely attainable through human words.[1] By contrast, in Scripture truth is always connected with God's person and work, never with abstract forms. In his high-priestly prayer Jesus says, 'And this is eternal life, that they may know you, the only true God, and Jesus Christ whom you have sent' (John 17:3). Thus, truth is the truth of God. The Father is the truth in the highest imaginable sense. The Bible attributes the same to the Son and to the Holy Spirit. 'God is "the truth," truth absolute, ultimate, eternal, in contradistinction from all that is relative, derived, partial, and temporal.'[2] This truth is very much attainable, because God himself has revealed it in human language.

Much as we admire the 'conservative' critique of the university, and much as we resonate with its warning about minds being closed, we cannot be satisfied to respond merely with an appeal to timeless forms and great books. The real problem, as we shall see, is that the departure from truth is a rebellion against God himself. Our closed minds are not just the unfortunate consequence of relativism, but of our blameworthy transgression against God's person and work. To open the mind again will require more than the ability to distinguish between opinion and knowledge.

[1] Plato, *Timaeus*, 28.
[2] John Murray, *Principles of Conduct* (Grand Rapids: Eerdmans, 1957), p. 125.

3

Our Mind and the Gospel

*In addition, the goodness of God appears as love when
it not only conveys certain benefits but God himself.*
—Herman Bavinck[1]

The Christian religion is simple: profound, but marvellously simple. It can be summarized in two great precepts: love God, love your neighbour. When asked by a local theological expert what the greatest commandment might be, Jesus spontaneously affirmed the answer from well-known words in the book of Deuteronomy: 'You shall love the Lord your God with all your heart and with all your soul and with all your might' (Deut. 6:5). He added that there was a second commandment like the first: 'You shall love your neighbour as yourself' (Lev 19:18). On these two, all of the law depends (Matt. 22:40).

---

[1] Herman Bavinck (1854–1921) was a Dutch Reformed theologian and churchman perhaps best known for his *Reformed Dogmatics* (Grand Rapids, MI: Baker Academic, 2008), 4 vols.

Using Our Mind

How do these two commandments relate to the Christian mind? Many children can remember their parents telling them, 'Use your head.' Some might have heard, 'Try to think; you have a good set of brains.' The idea behind this kind of language is that our minds are rational apparatuses that may have greater or lesser capacity to solve problems. In many Western countries standard tests exist to measure the ability of the brain to compute or to verbalize. Entrance to higher levels of education may depend on such test scores.

This view of the mind is quite different from the view found in the Bible. The English word 'mind' can translate a number of Hebrew or Greek words. In the Old Testament, most often the word 'mind' is a translation of the Hebrew for the *heart* (1 Sam. 9:20; 1 Kings 3:9, 12; 1 Chron. 22:19; Neh. 6:8; Job 28:36; Prov. 12:8). The heart in Scripture is the centre of our selves, of our personality. The word 'mind' occasionally translates the Hebrew words *spirit*, or *breath*, which are the enlivening principle that set human beings apart from non-humans (see 1 Chron. 22:19; Ezek. 11:6; 20:32). In the New Testament 'mind' often translates the Greek words for *spirit* or *understanding* (Rom. 7:23, 25; 11:34; 1 Cor. 1:10; 2:16; 14:14; 2 Thess. 2:2). It can also refer to *purpose* (intention) or *judgment* (Mark 5:15; Rom. 1:28; Eph. 2:3; 1 Pet. 3:8; Rev. 17:13).

One of the categories most often associated with the mind is *reason*. In Scripture reason often simply means an explanation or a cause, as in *the reason this happened is that* … (Gen. 47:13; Josh. 5:4; 1 Kings 11:27; Prov. 1:11; Luke 6:7; John 12:18; Acts 22:30). But it also can mean argument, as in the process of reasoning things out. One of the most familiar usages is Isaiah 1:18: 'Come now, let us reason together …' Here the Lord is saying, through his prophet, that if they will only think it through, there are certain causes for the misery of Israel. That can all change, again, if they will think it through. God's grace is such that if only the people would turn back to him he would change them and renew them. It is the gospel message in the Old Testament: 'Come, sit down, let me help you reason this thing out: you are on a destructive path, but you can change, for I am ready to forgive you' (see also James 3:17; Luke 9:47; Acts 19:8, 9). Reason can also simply refer to someone's mental normalcy. King Nebuchadnezzar temporarily lost his reason, under God's judgment (Dan. 4:33-37).

Notice two things. First, this reasoning process which discovers the gospel cannot be achieved alone. God must initiate it and must guide the entire process. Second, notice how much more holistic the idea of reasoning is than just brain capacity. Great learning is certainly approved in the Bible, but that is never associated with intellectual aptitude in the modern sense. Instead, the mind is a seat of understanding, the place of judgments, in short, the heart. It is a place for the cultivation of wisdom. In this book, then, when we use the term *mind* we will try to reflect this larger sense, including such things as intentions, spiritual aspirations, reasoning, and other capacities.

The New Testament records several times in which the two greatest commandments are quoted. In Mark and Matthew they are given in answer to the question from a specialist in the law. To the question, which is the most important of the commandments, Jesus answers these two, loving God and loving our neighbour. In Luke the answer is elicited from the inquirer. In all three accounts the word *mind* is added to the original list in the first commandment (Matt. 22:37; Mark 12:30; Luke 10:27). The Greek word is *dianoia*, meaning understanding. What are we to make of this? As is often the case with New Testament quotations of the Old, there is a certain amount of freedom in the details of these quotations. But it certainly means our thought world should be every bit as directed toward God in love as all other parts of ourselves.

The point of these categories within the first and greatest commandment is not to describe technical divisions in biblical anthropology. As with passages such as Hebrews 4:12 and 1 Thessalonians 5:23, the nouns are piled up, meaning the whole person. We are to love God with all of our being. The reason? God's remarkable faithfulness. In Deuteronomy 6 this grand law is prefaced by the words of the *Shema*:[1] 'Hear O Israel: The Lord our God, the Lord is one' (Deut. 6:4). The emphasis here is not so much that

---

[1] *Shema Yisrael* is a Jewish prayer, the centrepiece of the daily morning and evening prayer services. It is considered by some the most essential prayer in all of Judaism. An affirmation of God's singularity and kingship, its daily recitation is regarded by traditionally observant Jews as a biblical commandment.

God is a supreme being, which is true. It is not a statement defending monotheism, though it certainly implies that. It is rather a statement of God's exclusive faithfulness: the Lord our God (*Elohim*) is the only one who is rightly named LORD or *Jehovah*. There is only one covenant God, only one who has brought the people out of Egypt. The God of the Bible is not a local God, restricted to a particular town or mountain. God is not the best among many. Only this one God has saved his people.

Therefore we should love the Lord our God with all our heart, with all our soul and with all our might and mind. We should love him with every strain of our being, because he first loved us. Since only this God has loved us, we owe him exclusive and whole-souled love in return. To put it this way may sound rather cold and mechanical. But there is nothing perfunctory about God's love, nor should there be anything about ours in return.

The most astonishing aspect of God's love is its self-giving.

God's goodness is the greatest of his moral attributes. It is because God is good that he shows his love to undeserving sinful people. His goodness appears as grace when it is manifested to those who only deserve evil. And goodness appears as love when it not only conveys certain benefits *but God himself*.[1] This unspeakable gift is the costliest ever given, for it involved the death of the Son on the cross. The Christian religion is the only one whose God has wounds.

[1] See Bavinck, *Reformed Dogmatics, Vol. II, God and Creation*, p. 215.

Such love requires our loving response, with all our being, including our minds.

The second commandment is inseparable from the first. Every breakdown in human society stems from the primary loss of the love of God. The two commandments, love of God and love of neighbour, are inextricably joined. We cannot have love of neighbour without the love of God. Why is the sanctity of life so disregarded? Why has truth fallen in the street? According to Scottish theologian John Murray (1898–1975), it is because 'we have dragged God down to our level and have forgotten the incomparable in love —love to God with all the heart, and soul, and mind.'[1]

But Our Minds Are Darkened

From what we have said it must be abundantly clear that this whole-souled love for God, which includes the devotion of the mind, is a human impossibility. The Bible's diagnosis of our condition is rather severe, painfully realistic. 'For the mind that is set on the flesh is hostile to God, for it does not submit to God's law; indeed it cannot. Those who are in the flesh cannot please God' (Rom. 8:7, 8). This judgment on the human condition does not say nothing good can ever come of a human being. Nor does it say each human being is as bad as he possibly could be. It is saying that outside of Christ we are moving in the wrong direction. Indeed, we have minds set on the flesh. This means our base motivation is hostile to God. The dynamic for our living is inimical to God and to the things that matter most. Paul

[1] John Murray, 'The Christian Ethic,' p. 179.

puts it this way to the Ephesians: we once *lived* among the sons of disobedience, 'carrying out the desires of the body and the mind …' (Eph. 2:3).

So, while we may do certain good things, we cannot ultimately please God. To please him would require a perfect conformity to his will, and perfect motivation. Even the best persons are very far from honouring God. American theologian and philosopher Francis Schaeffer (1912–84) illustrated it this way. Suppose you are setting out to swim across the Pacific Ocean from California to Hawaii. The distance is about 4,000 kilometres. A normal swimmer might make it a couple of kilometres from the California coast before succumbing. A very strong swimmer might get a bit farther. But which one would get anywhere near Hawaii? Neither. If you are an average person, with some good qualities and some faults, how close are you to pleasing God? Even if you are a very good person, generous, full of integrity, are you any closer than the average person? This is very bad news.

Let us clarify something. By saying our minds are corrupt we don't mean they are incapable of functioning altogether. It's the direction, the motivation that have gone wrong, not the ability to calculate, to make certain judgments, and so forth. It means, however, that no matter how smart we may be, before coming to Christ we are not capable of rightly understanding the world, the nature of God, the meaning of the Bible, etc. An old professor of mine used to illustrate it this way. Suppose a man is using a brand new, well-functioning electric saw in his basement.

He is about to cut several wooden boards in order to make a floor. So he sets the dials on his saw and leaves the room for a minute. He returns and starts the machine. What he does not know is that while he was away his seven-year-old son came down and played with the dials. When the man started the machine it cut the boards all wrong.[1] The saw (the mind) is working just fine, except that the settings (the orientation of the mind) are askew. This means we can navigate all kinds of things in life just fine, but not who God is, how lost we are, and how to obtain eternal life.

But here is some good news. This same God we are so far from pleasing has provided another way to come to him besides moral reform. He has sent his only Son to live a life of perfect obedience, and to receive the full curse of God for sin, not his own but ours. Thus, Paul, after his severe diagnosis to the Ephesians, goes on to say, 'But God, being rich in mercy, because of the great love with which he loved us, even when we were dead in our trespasses, made us alive together with Christ—by grace you have been saved—and raised us up with him …' (Eph. 2:4-6). If you are a reader already convinced of this great truth, do not let these words cease to amaze you. And if you are not so convinced, let these words penetrate deep into your soul and astonish you with what God was willing to do for the sake of sinners. If we have but the slightest sense of our unworthiness, we will resonate with the words of the Welsh-born English poet George Herbert (1593–1633):

[1] Cornelius Van Til, *The Defense of the Faith*, 4th edition, ed. K. Scott Oliphint (Phillipsburg, NJ: P & R Publishing, 2008), pp. 97, 105.

Love bade me welcome. Yet my soul drew back
    Guilty of dust and sin.
But quick-eyed Love, observing me grow slack
    From my first entrance in,
Drew nearer to me, sweetly questioning,
    If I lacked any thing.

A guest, I answered, worthy to be here:
    Love said, You shall be he.
I the unkind, ungrateful? Ah my dear,
    I cannot look on thee.
Love took my hand, and smiling did reply,
    Who made the eyes but I?

Truth Lord, but I have marred them: let my shame
    Go where it doth deserve.
And know you not, says Love, who bore the blame?
    My dear, then I will serve.
You must sit down, says Love, and taste my meat:
    So I did sit and eat.[1]

So, then, our minds, and our whole selves, have been marred and have become incapable of reform. But God so loved us that he devised a way to repair all that was broken, and to start us on the journey to perfect love of this great Saviour.

---

[1] George Herbert, *The Works of George Herbert*, ed. F. E. Hutchinson (Oxford: Clarendon Press, 1967), p. 188.

4

The Content of Our Thinking: God

Thus, in order that the great nobility of our race (which distinguishes us from brute beasts) may not be buried beneath our own dullness of wit, it behoves us to recognize that we have been endowed with reason and understanding so that, by leading a holy and upright life, we may press on to the appointed goal of blessed immortality.

—John Calvin[1]

W hy have we been given our minds? The ancient Stoics thought it was to overcome the weaknesses of our emotions by understanding the world around us and to remind ourselves that virtue will always triumph over adversity. A more popular version of Stoicism is the proverb, 'mind over matter.' The Bible has an altogether different answer. We have been given our minds for the purpose of knowing God. At the dawn of human history,

[1] French theologian and leading Protestant reformer (1509–1564).

29

God created mankind after his own image (Gen. 1:26, 27). This is unique. We are neither demigods nor animals. A demigod would not be an image, but a partial original. The term image clearly tells us we are not God, but fully creatures. But neither are we mere animals, since we have properties not shared by the animal world. We do share certain properties with the animals, since we eat, we breathe, we reproduce, etc. But what distinguishes us from them is our ability to know God personally. We are rational beings whose minds can apprehend God.

Not That We Have Loved God

In the opening paragraphs of his highly influential book on Christian doctrine, *The Institutes of the Christian Religion*, John Calvin declares that all sound wisdom consists of two parts: the knowledge of God and of ourselves.[1] It is important to note that Calvin does not begin with the abstract notions of existence or being. He deliberately speaks of knowledge. Knowledge is personal, not primarily notional or theoretical. The entire *Institutes* develops this twofold truth. God is the originator of human thought as well as its object. Our knowledge is utterly dependent on God's, not the other way around. But yet we do have this remarkable capacity to know. Such a capacity is among God's most marvellous gifts to us. According to Calvin's understanding of Scripture's teaching on this subject, the reason we have so many remarkable gifts is so that we may more clearly see God: 'Then, by these benefits shed like dew

[1] John Calvin, *The Institutes of the Christian Religion*, I.i.1-2.

from heaven upon us, we are led as by rivulets to the spring itself.[1] Furthermore, our insufficiencies lead us to recognize God's great presence. In our state of wretchedness, we turn to God for solace. Why so? Because we understand from Scripture that God is good, and willing to forgive his wayward creatures. Because the pious mind 'is persuaded that he is good and merciful, it reposes in him with perfect trust, and doubts not that in his loving-kindness a remedy will be provided for all its ills.'[2]

Knowing God is an end in itself. In our day, when so many are struggling to find meaning and purpose, being able to claim a personal knowledge of Almighty God is an unspeakable privilege. We are not merely recommending knowing *about* God. That is marvellous, to be sure. So many people are wandering without purpose; so just knowing there is a God, and knowing certain things about him is a step in the right direction. Despite the decline in church attendance in the West, numbers of people still go to church and enjoy the services. In the hymns, the prayers, the sermons, they may discover a good deal about God.

Still, there is a world of difference between knowing *about* God and actually knowing him. He is the greatest good. Alas, there are many popular preachers today who advocate knowing God in order to get something from him—perhaps a better life, more self-confidence, greater happiness, etc. Scriptural support for this is taken from different places, always in isolation from the larger biblical

[1] Calvin, *Institutes*, I.i.1.
[2] Calvin, *Institutes*, I.ii.2.

picture. For example, the parable of the talents (Matt. 25:14-30) is taken as a formula for financial growth, rather than what it actually is, an illustration of the need to persevere in faith until the Lord returns.

It is legitimate to think that if we lead godly lives, God may bless us with a measure of security and health. But it is a travesty to make this into a norm. The Bible describes many people who are poor, physically unwell, victims of oppression, and though it offers them eternal hope and the joy of knowing God, it never promises about present, temporal relief from the 'sufferings of this present time' (Rom. 8:18). It's a delicate balance, for indeed the Lord cares deeply about our condition. And he wants the very best for us. The poor, Jesus declared, are blessed, for theirs is the kingdom. Those who mourn will be comforted (Matt. 5:3, 4). The Father knows our needs, and is not indifferent to them (Matt. 6:32). But there are priorities even greater than relief from our sufferings. The Lord wants us to find rest for our souls in fellowship with himself (Matt. 10:28-30). Jesus certainly fed the crowd miraculously. But he wearied of their wanting only food, not because he did not care about their hunger, but because there were greater benefits than food which they ought to have been pursuing. In John's Gospel Jesus stresses his complete adequacy by comparing himself to bread. 'I am the bread of life,' he declares. But he admonishes his listeners, 'Do not labour for the food that perishes, but for the food that endures to eternal life, which the Son of man will give to you' (John 6:27).

The most fundamental error in seeking God for what he can do for us is that it gets everything upside down. It imagines God loves us because we have potential. It imagines he will respond when we love him, when in reality it is quite the opposite: 'In this is love, not that we have loved God but that he first loved us and sent his Son to be the propitiation for our sins' (1 John 4:10). This is an astonishing statement. It goes against the grain of all human religion, of all our questing and searching and longing. Yes, we long to see God. But behind this longing, God is actually longing to see us! The reason? Love does not have a reason. But somehow, because of this love, God wants us for himself. He wants our friendship, our communion.

Effects of the Knowledge of God

Having said that knowing God is an end in itself, we can, of course, celebrate the effects this knowledge ought to have on us. It produces great benefits, all of which are centred on the Lord. True, there are secondary benefits, such as being cared for by God, and being protected by him under normal circumstances. If we seek God and his kingdom, life's necessities will be supplied to us by our provident heavenly Father (Matt. 6:33). Yet the primary benefits are circular, in the best sense: knowing God leads to better ways to know God! In his powerful study, *Knowing God*,[1] English theologian J. I. Packer (1926–) gives us four advantages to knowing God, all drawn out from the Old Testament book

[1] J. I. Packer, *Knowing God* (Downers Grove: Inter-Varsity Press, 1973), pp. 23-27.

of Daniel. Notice how little they have to do with prosperity, healing, self-image, and the like.

(1) *Those who know God have great energy for God.* In Daniel 11, we read that 'The people who know their God shall stand firm and take action' (Dan. 11:32). Packer notes that the faithful people recorded in this prophetic book were full of courage. This means they were compelled every so often to stand against the enormous pressures of the surrounding culture. When Nebuchadnezzar abolished the practice of prayer, under pressure from his advisors, Daniel went on publicly to pray three times a day (Dan. 6). For that he was sent to a den of lions, which he survived thanks to God's intervention. This great energy is not only in order to resist, but to lead in the right direction. Daniel had understood something about God's timetable from reading Jeremiah (Dan. 9:1, 2). There were to be seventy years of captivity. That drove him to prayer. He confessed the sins of his people, and asked God to turn away his anger (Dan. 9:3-19). His prayers were answered (Dan. 9:20-23). Packer asks if we have the energy for such praying; if we do not it is a sign that we 'scarcely know our God.'[1]

(2) *Those who know God have great thoughts of God.* Daniel was given access to the most privileged information about God and his ways. Throughout the book he tells kings what their dreams signified, and he predicts the future. He tells Nebuchadnezzar that he must be humiliated till he knows 'that the Most High rules the kingdom of men

[1] Packer, *Knowing God*, p. 24.

and gives it to whom he will' (Dan. 4:25; see also 5:21). We should remember that the massive Babylonian empire had engulfed tiny Palestine. And yet this one chosen vessel had a knowledge of God and his ways unparalleled by his captors. In one of his prayers, Daniel acknowledges the wisdom of God: 'he reveals deep and hidden things; he knows what is in the darkness, and the light dwells with him' (Dan 2:22). Again, Packer asks whether our understanding of God's grandeur keeps us 'awed and obedient' as it did Daniel?[1]

(3) *Those who know God show great boldness for God.* Similar to (1) above, yet here the emphasis is on taking intrepid risks for God's sake. Daniel and his friends needed to count the cost. Then they would decide regardless of the consequences, based on what was right. A poignant case in point is when Daniel and his three companions, Shadrach, Meshach, and Abednego refused to bow down before Nebuchadnezzar's image (Dan. 3). Their refusal meant being thrown into a blazing furnace. At their trial, they told the king, 'If this be so, our God whom we serve is able to deliver us from the burning fiery furnace … *but if not*, be it known to you, O king, that we will not serve your gods or worship the golden image that you have set up' (Dan. 3:17-18). Notice their confidence: God can do it, but if he does not, we will still act morally. The great Welsh preacher Dr Martyn Lloyd-Jones (1899–1981) equates this kind of courage with knowing what it is to be a Christian:

[1] Packer, *Knowing God*, p. 25.

In the long history of the Christian church, thinking of every revival and period of reformation, and the martyrs and confessors, there is only one explanation: those people knew what it was to be a Christian. They could defy tyrants without any fear; they could look into the face of death and say, 'It is well.' They were not afraid of men, of death, or even of hell, because they knew their position in the Lord Jesus Christ, and the result was that these people triumphed.[1]

Again, Packer affirms that by the test of this courage we may measure our knowledge of God.

(4) *Those who know God have great contentment in God.* Finally, there is a certain peace in knowing God. Such peace begins with the objective fact that we are justified by faith, and therefore we possess real peace, not so much the subjective feeling of peace, but rather the objective end of God's hostility towards us on account of our sins. Having been exonerated, we may be content, come what may, because God is at peace with us! But then we can know 'the peace of God' for ourselves (Phil. 4:7). Daniel's three friends knew this kind of confidence, and it enabled them to stand up to the powerful potentate and tell him, in effect, they are content whether they live or die. This, too, shows us what it means to know God.[2]

---

[1] Martyn Lloyd-Jones, 'Not of the World,' *O Love that Will Not Let Me Go: Facing Death with Courageous Confidence in God*, ed. Nancy Guthrie (Wheaton: Crossway, 2011), p. 35.

[2] J. I. Packer, *Knowing God*, p. 27.

5

The Content of Our Knowledge: Our Neighbour

Before you can give this neighbour-love, you need to receive it. Only if you see that you have been saved graciously by someone who owes you the opposite will you go out into the world looking to help absolutely anyone in need.

—Timothy Keller[1]

I f the first and greatest commandment is to love God, the second is 'like unto it.' In his magnificent treatise *The Freedom of a Christian* (1520) German reformer Martin Luther (1483–1546) joins two themes that might at first seem contradictory: (1) A Christian is lord of all, completely free of everything. (2) A Christian is a servant, completely attentive to the needs of all.[2] The first theme became the Reformation call for coming to God by faith, and not

[1] Timothy J. Keller (1950–) is an American pastor, theologian, and Christian apologist.

[2] Martin Luther, *The Freedom of a Christian*, tr. Mark D. Tranvik (Minneapolis: Fortress Press, 2008), p. 50.

through works. Nothing external, no prayer, no fasting, no abstinence can lord it over us, nothing human can earn us the presence of God, and thus nothing human can claim our allegiance. Only his word can bring us to God, as it brings to the soul 'life, truth, light, peace, righteousness, salvation, joy, liberty, wisdom, power, grace, glory, and every other blessing imaginable.'[1] And the only way to obtain this blessing is through faith, the faith that frees us from the law, the faith that honours God, and the faith that unites the soul to Christ.[2] But now this primary relationship with God is necessarily linked to the service of our neighbour. We live, not for ourselves, but for all other people.[3] 'Given the abundance of our faith, our life and works become a surplus to be used freely in the service of the neighbour.'[4] In his unique way of putting it, Luther says, 'Through faith we are caught up beyond ourselves into God. Likewise, through love we descend beneath ourselves through love to serve our neighbour.'[5]

Loving Our Brethren

Luther has captured a profound biblical insight. The love of God, if it is genuine, should always be accompanied by the love of our neighbour. The apostle John drives the point home this way: 'We know that we have passed out of death into life, because we love the brothers' (1 John 3:14). He goes

[1] Martin Luther, *Freedom of a Christian*, p. 53.
[2] Martin Luther, *Freedom of a Christian*, pp. 59-65.
[3] Martin Luther, *Freedom of a Christian*, p. 79.
[4] Martin Luther, *Freedom of a Christian*, p. 81.
[5] Martin Luther, *Freedom of a Christian*, pp. 88-89.

on to drive the knife in, by asking, 'But if anyone has the world's goods and sees his brother in need, yet closes his heart against him, how does God's love abide in him?' (1 John 3:17). Our Lord puts it poignantly by saying, 'Truly I say to you, as you did it to one of the least of these my brothers, you did it to me' (Matt. 25:40).

Thus, to know God issues in the knowledge of our neighbour, particularly when he is in need. Many implications flow from this connection. Knowledge of our neighbour means drawing close enough to him or to her that we have a sense of their gifts and their needs. The Bible has extensive instruction on how to love our neighbour. Romans 12:9–13:10 contains rich instructions on how to approach our different neighbours in order to love them. The section concludes with a reminder that love is expressed by obedience to God's law: 'therefore love is the fulfilling of the law' (Rom. 13:10). So the Christian mind is a commitment to loving God and loving our fellow human beings.

One remarkable feature about the Lord's call to love our neighbour is that he speaks of the duty in terms of a *new* commandment (John 13:34; 1 John 2:8). This may come as a surprise, since, as we have seen, the commandment to love our neighbour is found way back in Leviticus 19:17. What could be new about the commandment? It is that we now must practise such love in and through Jesus Christ. In his farewell speech to the disciples on the eve of his passion the Lord told them, 'A new commandment I give to you, that you love one another: just as I have loved you, you also are to love one another.' And he adds, 'By this all people will know that you are my disciples, if you have love for one another' (John 13:34, 35). John reiterates this directive in his first letter: 'At the same time, it is a new commandment that I am writing you, which is true in him and in you' (1 John 2:8).

Jesus indeed showed us the consummate way of love. Though the Creator, he became an infant. Though Lord of all, he became a servant. Though the source of life, he died the death of a criminal. Though very God of very God, he remains human forever. Such love is unsearchable. How can he command it of his people? Only because with the demand comes the grace to accomplish it—not perfectly, not all at once, but in reality. It is not certain that those of us who are Christians are fully aware both of the privilege and the responsibility of this new commandment. But we must put our minds to it and think of ways we can exhibit the new commandment to love.

Extending Mercy

One of the challenges for us as we fix our minds on the conditions of our neighbour is how to respond to their needs. When we think of world poverty we often are stunned by the numbers. Over three billion people on our planet live on $2.50 or less per day. More than two billion have no bank account. One in nine persons suffers from chronic undernourishment. Though many live in developing countries it may come as a surprise to learn that one in seven people in North America are classified as poor. More than half a million of them are homeless.

Faced with these numbers we feel helpless. When I am walking around in a large city, I often see destitute people lying on the sidewalk. My immediate reaction is to hand them a little cash. This can be all right, but in most cases it does nothing to relieve the poor person. So then, I think to myself, there are organizations and churches who specialize in this kind of care, so I don't need to worry about it. Neither approach is quite right.

The better way is to get involved in poverty relief, preferably through a church or a Christian charity that approaches it systematically. The very first priority is to develop a properly biblical view of mercy. The very essence of the gospel is to present God's grace to a needy people. Jesus' first sermon in Nazareth proclaimed, 'The Spirit of the Lord is upon me, because he has anointed me to proclaim good news to the poor' (Luke 4:18). God's mercy toward us is unconditional. It does not stop to ask, why are you in this state, before proffering grace on us. When the Samaritan had compassion on the victim on the Jericho road he did not ask diagnostic questions, but went ahead and helped the man. This does not mean questions should not be asked eventually. But we should start by imitating God's ways with us: 'Having loved his own who were in the world, he loved them to the end' (John 13:1).

After this, the best organizations will need to continue with a sound diagnosis of the problem. Poverty can have several causes. Some poverty is caused by injustice or oppression. Some is caused by some sort of major disaster, such as a famine or earthquake, or by a minor one, such as loss of employment or an unexpected pregnancy. Some poverty is caused by bad decisions. Often these three work in combination.

The best organization follows with the appropriate plan of action for each kind of need. Often the starting point must be immediate assistance. Direct relief meets the most obvious needs: food, clothing, shelter, and the like. Sometimes legal defence may be necessary, or counselling may be needed. But the relief organization cannot stop there. It must think of the next step, which is some kind of transformation, so that the problems will not recur. The further steps may take the form of language training, or help with job creation. Some homeless shelters will take victims in for a year or two, and will seek to train them to become more self-sufficient. But the final step is much more long term. There is a need for social reform.[1] Poverty and homelessness are the result of structures, as well as individual circumstances. Thus Christians ought to do their part in influencing policies, educational systems, police protection, and so forth. When our minds examine this larger picture, we are more likely to have confidence in the gospel's answer to these massive problems.

Of course, loving our neighbour involves more than mercy to the destitute. Often our neighbour is literally the person next door, or even the person living with us. How may we help them with their needs? From offering to

---

[1] These three steps are suggested by Timothy Keller, *Ministries of Mercy: The Call of the Jericho Road* (Phillipsburgh, NJ: P & R Publishing, 1997), pp. 181-90.

babysit their children, to helping them with housework, to doing errands. These mundane activities are a part of loving our neighbour. Of course, none of us is sufficient to meet the need of everyone. We may only be able to concentrate on one or two people. When Jesus told his disciples that the poor would always be with them (Matt. 26:11; Mark 14:7), he was not encouraging a spirit of indifference. No, he was reminding them of their priorities: Jesus first, then the world's problems.

It might be objected here that we are confusing the gospel with social action. It's a legitimate concern. There have been times in the history of the church where the concern for the poor and the disenfranchised has obscured the larger purposes of God for his people, and the comprehensive nature of their salvation. At one point, a movement known as the *social gospel* engaged in such a confusion.[1] That was one extreme. But the opposite extreme is so to emphasize the saving of the soul that a concern for the whole person, including their social and psychological needs, can be ignored. Such a dichotomy is foreign to the New Testament. The heart of the gospel is reconciliation with God, being right with the Creator. Everything pertaining to human life flows from this, our entrance into heaven, certainly, but also what the Bible calls *sanctification*, the renovation of all of life under the lordship of Christ (Col. 1:15-20).

---

[1] Its most notable representatives were from North America at the turn of the twentieth century: Richard Ely, Josiah Strong, and Walter Rauschenbusch.

Caveat

One often hears in popular talks or sermons that we have three, not two commandments here: to love God, to love our neighbour, and to love ourselves. In an age where self-love permeates the atmosphere, this becomes appealing. But it is quite wrong. There are only two commandments. Loving our neighbour is to be practised 'as yourself', meaning, we ought to extend love to our neighbour with the same kind of care and attention we give to ourselves. If I become ill I go to get help. If I am in need, I go to find assistance. Well, I should care as much about my neighbour's needs as I do about my own. It may be true that not every person loves himself. In a fallen world, we find self-hatred as well as self-love. But surely Leviticus is not opening up that kind of detail. The book is pointing to the ordinary, the normal. We typically invest a good deal in ourselves. We ought to do at least as much for our neighbour.

6

The Source for Right Thinking

To some extent, looking back, I think evangelical Christians had been closer to the rationalists than we should have been and we found it hard to articulate a way of talking about truth without falling into something like a claim of exhaustive knowledge.—Michael J. Ovey[1]

The next part of our consideration follows from what has been said so far. If knowing God, accompanied by knowing our neighbour, is the object of our mind's attention, then where do we go in order to nurture our mind? No surprise. It is, of course, to that same God. How may we do this?

God Gets Through

Unless God discloses himself to us we can have no assurance that our knowledge of him or of our neighbour is true.

---

[1] Michael J. Ovey (1958–2017) was a British Anglican clergyman, academic, and former lawyer. From 2007 until his death, he was Principal of Oak Hill College, a conservative evangelical theological college in London.

Because we are creatures any knowledge of God will have to be mediated. Mediation does not have to mean distortion, or even alteration. The reason we may be sure that what is revealed to us can reach us as God intended is that he is the Creator, the Lord of all, and he wants us to know the truth. He made us so that we could know him. Most Christians acknowledge the Creator-creature distinction, but not all of them realize its full implications.

Have we thought about how it is that God, who is utterly transcendent, can communicate with his creatures, particularly with humans, who are finite beings? Allow me a small technical detour. Two typical false answers will give an idea of the problem. The first is that we simply cannot know anything true, at least we cannot know what God thinks. Everything we know is *equivocal*, approximate. A sceptic will boldly state that there is no way out of this prison. There are many forms of scepticism, and none can be entirely consistent or it could not affirm its views with any degree of certainty. One of the most consistent sceptics was Pierre Charron (1541–1603). In his *Les Trois Vérités* (*The Three Truths*, 1594) he argued that the nature and existence of God are unknowable. Because God is so great he is inaccessible, except to blind faith.[1] Despite his appeals to faith, Charron was widely viewed by his critics as

---

[1] Charron, curiously, meant this as a defence of the Roman Catholic Church, against the Protestants. If we cannot know God by reason, we can take refuge in the Roman Church, whose authority could compensate for human weakness. As well, we can practice high ethical standards, simply because we should.

simply a sceptic. They wanted to know how someone who does not believe in reason could make such a *reasonable* case against it!

The second unhelpful answer is in the opposite direction. It says, in order to know the truth we must know it in exactly the way God knows it. This is sometimes known as *univocal* knowledge. The argument here says that this is the only alternative to scepticism. Certainly, no Christian thinker would say that somehow we are God, even partly God. That would devolve into pantheism or into pure rationalism. But they might argue that unless we have concepts common to God and to man we cannot avoid scepticism. Duns Scotus (*c.* 1266–1308) held such a view. Before we can have a concept of God, there must be a common univocal concept, that is, common both to God and man, that allows us to build a bridge from the creature to the Creator.[1] His critics worried that he had jettisoned the full transcendence of God. Even if we say we have concepts in common with God we are devolving into somehow being God-like, which is unacceptable.

Is there a third way? Can we ever know truly, that is, as God wants us to know, without usurping his place? Yes. The reason is that the Creator has made us after his image,

---

[1] Duns Scotus, *God and Creatures: The Quodlibetal Questions*, tr. F. Alluntis & A. B. Wolter (Princeton: Princeton University Press, 1983). John Duns, commonly called Duns Scotus, was a Scottish Catholic priest and Franciscan friar, university professor, philosopher, and theologian. He is one of the three most important philosopher-theologians of Western Europe in the High Middle Ages, together with Thomas Aquinas and William of Ockham.

and is able to communicate with us because he is all-powerful. The Lord can get through to his servant, as a father can speak to his children. Certainly, God's knowledge is original, creative, all-sufficient, and exhaustive, while human knowledge will always be derivative, re-creative, dependent, and finite. Yet such distinctions do not in any way prevent us from knowing truly. Francis Schaeffer was fond of saying we can know truly but not exhaustively. Dutch-American Christian philosopher and theologian Cornelius Van Til (1895–1987) said we could know by analogy.[1] By this he meant our thoughts are God's thoughts, only at a creaturely level.

There is a remarkable confirmation of this understanding of the relationship between divine and human knowledge in the story of Moses' call to lead Israel out of bondage in Egypt (Exod. 3–4). God reveals himself to Moses in the burning bush on Mount Horeb (Exod. 3:2). The text tells us a flame of fire burned out of the midst of the bush, and that though the bush was burning it was not consumed. Several Protestant denominations which trace their roots back to the Reformation of the sixteenth century have adopted the symbol of the burning bush. To them it signified that, though the fires of persecution may burn strongly, the people of God cannot be consumed or destroyed. The reason for that is God's protection of them.

Moses, perhaps understandably, raises several objections to his being the one chosen by God to lead his people.

---

[1] Cornelius Van Til liked to say we think by analogy. See his *Defense of the Faith*, pp. 62-73.

The first is, 'Why me?' To Moses' question, 'Who am I that I should go to Pharaoh?' God answers, 'But I will be with you,' to which he adds that he will bring them to the very mountain where this conversation is taking place (Exod. 3:11-12). Moses next raises the objection that he is not sure by what name to call this God who would summon the people through him. Then comes one of the most unique and powerful revelations in all of Scripture: 'God said to Moses, "I AM WHO I AM." And he said "Say this to the people of Israel, 'I AM has sent me to you'"' (Exod. 3:14). The Hebrew here is just four consonants (Hebrew has no vowels) which spell out the name of God (YHWH—sometimes rendered 'Jehovah' or 'Yahweh'). In the New Testament, particularly in John's Gospel, Jesus often refers to himself as the 'I am' (John 6:35; 8:12; 10:9, 10; 11:25; 12:46; 14:6; 15:1). Then God assures Moses that he will be enabled to work miraculous signs and wonders, which will include awe-inspiring signs of judgment (Exod. 3:19–4:10).

Moses objects one more time, pleading that he is a poor speaker (Exod. 4:10). Now, here, God gives him an answer which I believe can serve as the basis for our assurance that his revelation really does get through: 'Then the LORD said to him, "Who has made man's mouth? Who makes him mute, or deaf, or seeing, or blind? Is it not I, the LORD? Now therefore go, and I will be with your mouth and teach you what you shall speak"' (Exod. 4:11, 12). To put it simply, cannot God, who made mankind with hearing and sight and speech, not communicate with him what he wants, when he wants?

Over and over, the prophets tell the people, 'thus says the LORD,' and proceed to speak in human language. If we claim he is too far away, or inaccessible, then the Bible reminds us that 'The word is near you, in your mouth and in your heart' (Rom. 10:8; Deut. 30:14). God gets through. Our minds respond.

Covenant Condescension

The relationship of God to mankind, which generates knowledge in us, is rightly termed *covenantal*. A covenant is a contract between two parties. In the case of God and mankind this contract is not between two equal parties. God is 'high and lifted up,' the One 'who inhabits eternity, whose name is Holy' (Isa. 57:15). He is the Creator, we are creatures. He is infinite, we are finite. No matter how hard they might try to find God by searching, they will always be bound by their creaturely nature. In addition, since the fall, humans are corrupt. Not only can they not attain to God's truth, but they will find ways to distort it. So the only hope is for God to take the initiative. The *Westminster Confession of Faith* describes this relationship beautifully:

> The distance between God and the creature is so great, that although reasonable creatures do owe obedience unto him as their Creator, yet they could never have any fruition of him as their blessedness and reward, but by some voluntary condescension on God's part, which he hath been pleased to express by way of covenant (7.1).

There is a good deal going on here. Notice the language: 'by some voluntary condescension on God's part.' The word *condescension* may sound patronizing to modern ears. What it means here is that God waives his privilege as the glorious Creator in order to show himself to us. It is the same thought Paul expresses about Jesus' incarnation: 'though he was in the form of God, [he] did not count equality with God a thing to be grasped, but made himself nothing, taking the form of a servant, being born in the likeness of men' (Phil. 2:6, 7). This kind of condescension deserves careful thought. Neither the *Confession* nor Paul are suggesting that God could or would give up his divine nature, nor the second person of the Trinity his equality with the Father as a deity. That would be an impossibility. If God is less than God, he is no longer God. But it means he was willing to give up the privileges of his station, by adding humanity to himself, and thus rendering himself vulnerable. It helps to remember that Christ is one person but with two natures, divine and human. It's a grand mystery, one we do not have to solve in order to accept and believe.

In any case, this condescension on God's part is 'by way of covenant.' The covenant is that gracious act of God whereby he calls his people to himself. And he is able to do that because, in his mercy, he provided a way to atone for the sins of his people. In response his people owe him faith followed by obedience. So the covenant idea is this contract of unequal parties in order to redeem the people of God. The covenant reality is a successive unfolding of such contracts, beginning with Adam, and being renewed with Abraham, and progressively disclosed until its fullest manifestation in the New Covenant, centring in Jesus Christ.

One more detail should not go unnoticed. The *Confession* calls it a *voluntary* condescension. God did not have to do this. Especially since the fall he does not owe us anything. The very nature of grace is that it stems from God's loving decision, not from any kind of necessity. It changes our whole outlook when we realize that God did not have to save, nor even reveal himself to us. Instead, he was moved by love to make the very costly decision to save us. This should induce us to praise him. The great hymn of Charles Wesley (1707–88) captures well the spirit of such praise:

> Love divine, all loves excelling,
>> Joy of heaven to earth come down;
> Fix in us Thy humble dwelling;
>> All Thy faithful mercies crown!
> Jesus, Thou art all compassion,
>> Pure unbounded love Thou art;
> Visit us with Thy salvation;
>> Enter every trembling heart.
>
> Come, Almighty to deliver,
>> Let us all Thy grace receive;
> Suddenly return, and never,
>> Nevermore Thy temples leave.
> Thee we would be always blessing,
>> Serve Thee as Thy hosts above,
> Pray and praise Thee without ceasing,
>> Glory in Thy perfect love.

7

Refusing the Truth

He was an embittered atheist (the sort of atheist who does not so much disbelieve in God as personally dislike him).[1]

The question must now be raised, *Why does not everyone acknowledge and receive this divine covenantal revelation?* The Bible's answer is that we don't want it. Paul makes the point forcefully at the beginning of his letter to the Romans. Everyone knows God (1:19-21). Not just about him, but we know God himself. There is nothing unclear about God's revelation to us. Everyone sees him, in his attributes, the way he is. And yet, as Paul also tells us, this perception did not lead to a proper honouring of the Creator, but to his denial. He puts it in the strongest terms: 'For although they knew God, they did not honour him as God or give thanks to him, but they became futile in their thinking' (Rom. 1:21).

[1] Spoken of George Orwell (Eric Arthur Blair, 1903–50), an English novelist and essayist, journalist and critic, famous for his novels *Animal Farm* (1945) and *Nineteen Eighty-four* (1949).

Dishonouring God

We ought to pause over these words. Paul is not saying we know there is some large force out there. He is not even saying we know there must be a God. His language is as strong as it could be. We know God, the real God who is there. We know him from his revelation in the creation. We may put it more starkly: unbelievers know God; they really do. The thoughtful reader may be asking at this point, 'But then, why do they not acknowledge it? Can we really say of a Richard Dawkins or a Friedrich Nietzsche,[1] that they know God?' This text affirms that very thing. We are faced with the undeniable truth: 'The heavens declare the glory of God, and the sky above proclaims his handiwork' (Psa. 19:1). The psalm is not saying, *for those who wish to see it*, God may be discerned. It is there for everyone to see. It goes on to say, 'Day to day pours out speech, and night to night reveals knowledge. There is no speech, nor are there words, whose voice is not heard' (Psa. 19:2-3). The knowledge of God is unavoidable.

The reason we don't acknowledge this awareness of God is because we choose to process the knowledge wrongly. The text from Paul's letter to the Romans says it in a number of ways. We suppress the truth (1:18). We refuse to honour God or give him thanks (1:21). We have become futile in our thinking, our hearts are darkened; we have exchanged the glory of God for the worship of the creature (1:21-23).

---

[1] Friedrich Nietzsche (1844–1900) was a German philosopher and cultural critic whose work has exerted a profound influence on modern intellectual history.

In a word, we refuse the knowledge we have. Of course, it won't go away, so that there will always be a tension in our awareness, as long as we mount our attack on the presence of God.

Speaking personally, I have to confess that it took me some time to accept that I had not simply been ignorant of God but hostile towards him. I had thought of myself as a 'seeker,' one who was able to identify the object of my search and move on to a deeper understanding of God. But that was not so.

Some of the more honest philosophical authors help us to see that our reasons for arriving at certain conclusions are not disinterested. For example, Aldous Huxley (1894–1963), perhaps best known as the author of *Brave New World* (1932) and *The Doors of Perception* (1954), was a sceptic—though he thought there might be hope for the world through the use of mind-altering drugs! In a most candid essay, *Ends and Means*, Huxley makes a startling admission. His view that life was meaningless was motivated, not by an honest appraisal of the world, but by not wanting the world to have a meaning. It was easy for him to find reasons for life's meaninglessness once he had made that choice. But it was indeed a choice. He called it 'vincible ignorance.' He went on to say, 'We don't know because we don't want to know.' His philosophy of meaninglessness was for the purpose of liberating him from conventional morals, not because he thought his philosophy was true.[1]

---

[1] Aldous Huxley, *Ends and Means*, 6th edition (New York: Harper & Brothers, 1939), pp. 314-15.

Huxley is not alone in such candour. Sir Kenneth Clark (1903–83), the well-known art historian and host of the television series *Civilisation*, was at best an agnostic. That almost changed. He recounts a religious experience he had when in the Church of San Lorenzo. For a moment he felt a kind of heavenly joy. He felt 'the finger of God.' Then he makes a remarkable admission. He found that he was not able to confess that he had been wrong all his life. Although his life was far from blameless, he says he could not change course. If he did, his family might think him mad. So he simply tried to forget the experience, and he largely did, though it took some time.[1] The point here is not that Clark did or didn't have some kind of real experience. Rather, it is to note the deliberate way he chose to suppress what had happened to him.

Examples abound. The sceptical philosopher David Hume (1711–76), who provided so much fodder to the denial of miracles and the rejection of objectivity, looked into the abyss of nihilism, and decided it wasn't worth accepting its logical implications. So he stopped worrying and played backgammon with his friends instead.

Most of us do not have the stature of a Huxley, a Clark, or a Hume. But the manoeuvre is the same. When the abundant evidence for God, indeed the undeniable reality of God, presents itself, it becomes inconvenient for us to own up to it. The cost is too high.

This kind of moral revulsion is of our whole person, including the mind. When we sin, it is not simply our 'lower

[1] Kenneth Clark, *The Other Half: A Self-Portrait* (New York: Harper & Row, 1977), pp. 237-39.

selves,' or our passions that succumb. Our thinking can and does transgress. Theologians call it the *noetic effects of sin* (from the Greek word *nous*, often translated 'mind'). The only way to change our posture toward God is to experience repentance, a change of our entire disposition. The mind has a key role in repentance (in Greek, *metanoia*, is literally a 'change of the *nous*'). God calls people everywhere to repent (Acts 17:20). And they do so by the grace of the one who calls them. Only then may they begin to use their minds properly.

The Dynamics of Doubt

It is irrational not to believe. Yet unbelief is far more than simply a refusal to accept a reasonable proposition. So many appeals to theistic proofs fail to persuade because they cannot appeal to the requirements for proof. Books on such topics as 'evidence that demands a verdict,' or 'answers to Bible difficulties' abound. But how effective are they? Often their hidden assumption is that if we can only demonstrate the reasonableness of the Christian faith, then people will of necessity embrace it. But that assumption is not a biblical one. The so-called father of modern philosophy, René Descartes (1596–1650), thought he could cast aside all ideas that had no rational basis. He aimed 'to reach certainty; to cast aside the loose earth and sand so as to come upon a rock or clay.'[1] His famous 'rock of indubitability' was the thinking self, summarized by the Latin phrase

---

[1] René Descartes, *Discourse on Method*, in *Selected Philosophical Writings*, tr. John Cottingham & Robert Stoothoff (Cambridge: Cambridge University Press, 1988), 3/29, p. 34.

cogito ergo sum ('I think therefore I am'). Unfortunately, however, Descartes never thought to establish the authority of human reason, let alone its nature. Today, Descartes' foundationalism is rarely accepted. It is seen to lack the proper framework which makes reason credible. Sadly, some of the apologetical methods that proclaim Christianity as reasonable are equally unconvincing because they too lack the evidence for the credibility of reason.

The Christian faith is indeed rational, but not by Cartesian[1] standards. The ultimate standard for rationality must be God's. His thoughts are not inaccessible to us, but they can only be truly recognized when we bow before the Divine Thinker. The psalmist puts it this way:

> How precious to me are your thoughts, O God!
> How vast is the sum of them! (Psa. 139:17)

In order to receive biblical rationality we must bow down before God's own thoughts and then reform our own thought-world. The psalmist goes on to say,

> Search me, O God, and know my heart!
> Try me and know my thoughts!
> And see if there be any grievous way in me,
> and lead me in the way everlasting! (Psa. 139:23, 24)

According to the biblical view, human thought is only valid as it begins with the worship of God, and then asks that he purify our own thinking. This is the farthest thing from mindlessness. It is the most rational approach we

---

[1] Cartesian = relating to Descartes and his ideas.

could make, because it begins with God's own rationality and fully recognizes our dependence on him for our own thinking.

Thus, doubt is much more than the inability to solve a puzzle. It is the attempt to build up our knowledge autonomously, without a recognition of God's ultimate rationality. Doubt is characterized by false ideas of who God is, and of his ways. There are many examples of different kinds of doubters in the Bible. One thinks of King Saul, who would not conduct warfare in the way the Lord had prescribed, out of fear of the people (1 Sam. 15:24). One thinks of Pontius Pilate who publicly washed his hands of the trial over which he presided, out of fear of the people, even when he knew perfectly well that Jesus was innocent of all the charges against him (Matt. 27:24). There is the frightening story of the rich man who oppressed Lazarus, and later, when it was too late, asked Abraham to make a special intervention to warn his brothers, only to be told that they have Moses and the prophets, and that they would not believe in a miracle if they didn't believe in the Bible (Luke 16:19-31). In all these cases there were sufficient reasons to believe, but the moral courage to do so was missing.

The converse is true. The very first believer following the death of Jesus was a Gentile soldier. In Mark's powerful account of the crucifixion we are told that when the centurion saw the way Jesus breathed his last, he declared, 'Truly this man was the Son of God!' (Mark 15:39). How did he know? My guess is that this professional soldier had seen a good number of deaths, many of them accompanied by intense anguish and pain. Jesus suffered greatly, but he was always in control (John 10:18). We don't know how much more the soldier may have known about Jesus, but it was clearly the evidence of his God-like manner of dying that convinced the centurion. Some, such as the Philippian jailer, needed little additional evidence than the singing of God's praises, the earthquake, and then the reassuring words of his Christian prisoners to receive the word of God by faith (Acts 16:25-31). Others, perhaps such as Nicodemus, and certainly the disciples, took longer to come to faith and required more evidence. They may have measured the cost of believing and carefully weighed the issues involved before committing themselves to Christ. But the point is this: receiving the rational truth of the gospel is not only a matter of solving a conundrum, but of a willingness to yield to its gracious authority.

8

Faith and Reason

Crede ut intelligas [Believe in order that you may understand].

—Augustine

In worldly religions and worldly philosophies human beings look up, or look within, hoping to find meaning, or even power. There is a religious need in every person, and when it is not satisfied it looks, sometimes desperately, for some connection with a greater reality. And what does one find? If one is honest, not a great deal. To his friend Horatio, Hamlet famously remarks,

> There are more things in heaven and earth, Horatio,
> Than are dreamt of in your philosophy.[1]

The contrast could not be more stark between these worldly searches and biblical religion. The religion of the Bible is the result of God's reaching down to us, culminating in the incarnation of Jesus Christ, very God of very God.

[1] William Shakespeare, *Hamlet*, 1.5.

Faith

If all revelation in general, and the Bible in particular, is truly God's self-disclosure, then how are we to receive it? How may we put our Christian minds to the task of 'rightly handling the word of truth' (2 Tim. 2:15)? Is there any place for the exercise of our reason? There is only one proper answer to that question—by *faith*.

But what does faith mean, and how does it relate to our capacities to receive anything at all from God's revelation?

Faith emanates from the deepest recesses of the human heart. Why we believe is 'so deeply hidden in the life of the soul and so closely interwoven with the finest and most tender fibres of the human heart that it almost eludes our own perception and even more that of others.'[1] *Almost!* Why do we believe? What is it about faith that makes us willing to sacrifice everything for the sake of its object?

Faith is the only way to be free from the prison walls of pure subjectivism. Its fundamental characteristic is to lift empty hands and receive God's gift. Faith is trust, but it is informed trust. The Protestant tradition defines faith as consisting of three components, *knowledge*, *assent* and *trust*. Faith begins with an understanding of its object. In the case of Christianity that would be Jesus Christ as he is presented in the gospel. Faith also must include an element of assent, or agreement to the truth of its object. It is not enough to know the content of our faith, but we must believe it to be true. There are, sadly, many people

---

[1] Herman Bavinck, *Reformed Dogmatics, Vol. I, Prolegomena*, p. 503.

who know the content of the Christian worldview but who cannot accept it as true. Trust is the third necessary component of true faith. There are those, sadly, who know the Christian gospel to be true but who will not entrust themselves to Jesus Christ.

These three components cannot be quantified. Faith, our Lord taught us, can be as small as a grain of mustard seed but still be authentic (Matt. 17:20). Or it may appear robust but in fact be rootless and fruitless (Matt. 13:5-6). All depends on the way faith is nourished.

> It is possible of course to have little knowledge and considerable assurance, but that is because faith has nourished itself richly even on relatively limited knowledge of a great Saviour. Correspondingly, it is possible to have much knowledge and little assurance; that is because faith has starved itself by failing to feed on the knowledge it has.[1]

In Protestant theology the role of reason, or the intellect, has been largely esteemed. By means of the intellect we can make certain evaluations of our faith commitments. We may even change our minds. What, then, is reason? It is simply the human capacity to form judgments and make inferences.[2] At one level, that is simply a description of what reason does. It is a simple operation. The operation might be valid, but the conclusion quite wrong. For example, you

---

[1] Sinclair B. Ferguson, 'The Reformation and Assurance,' *Banner of Truth*, April 2017, p. 21.

[2] Text books on reason and logic abound. The above definition of reason is from John Frame, *Doctrine of the Knowledge of God* (Phillipsburg, NJ: P & R Publishing, 1987), p. 329.

might think a person is ignoring you because he doesn't like you. People who don't like me ignore me. But the person might just be shy. The operation was correct but it was based on a false premise. So, at another level, reason should have a normative character. 'This is quite reasonable' should mean, the use of reasoning is sound all the way through. That is the way we use the word most of the time.

How do I know I have really believed in Jesus Christ as he is presented in the Bible? How do I know I have not just had a good feeling, or simply embraced Christian words and customs? In part, the answer is that reason ought to provide a warrant for our belief. In the best theological tradition, faith and reason are not in conflict, but work together. For example, it is quite reasonable to require evidence for faith. When Jesus appeared to some of his disciples after his resurrection, Thomas, who was not with them, declared, 'Unless I see in his hands the mark of the nails, and place my finger into the mark of the nails, and place my hand into his side, I will never believe' (John 20:25). A week later he was given just such an opportunity. And when he saw the risen Christ, he confessed, 'My Lord and my God!' (20:28). Notice that Jesus did not deny him the opportunity to test the evidence (though it's not sure Thomas actually did put his hand in his wounds). Notice too that he praised those who could believe without having seen him (verse 29). We must be careful here. Jesus is not celebrating 'blind' faith. In the very next passage, the apostle John explains that the many signs recorded in his Gospel were written for the very purpose of leading readers to faith (20:30, 31). Throughout the Bible there are all kinds of helps which provide reasons for faith. Nevertheless, faith ought not be reduced to merely agreeing with a series of propositions. At some point there has to be *trust*, a receiving of, and resting in, the truth. We need to entrust ourselves to Jesus Christ, 'the way, and the truth, and the life' (John 14:6).

Reason

If faith must be reasonable, reason must be faithful! Many discussions go awry because *reason* is left undefined. The seventeenth-century Puritan theologian John Owen is most helpful here. He compares right thinking with spiritual-mindedness which is focused on Christ. Owen makes a good deal of the illustration Jesus used of the well of living water from which a person draws life-giving nourishment. Owen sternly warns his readers of many operations of the mind that have the appearance of being spiritual but which have no substance. Unless there is a constant renewal of the mind, beginning with conversion, then its activities will be barren. But when we are properly renewed, everything takes on a deep and rich meaning.[1]

One distinction, possibly originating with Martin Luther, is helpful. Reason is either *magisterial* or *ministerial*. If reason is magisterial, it stands above everything, much like the magistrate who has authority over his subjects. In this view, reason is able to judge what is true or admissible. If reason is ministerial, then it is a servant.

[1] Owen, *Grace and Duty of Being Spiritually Minded*, pp. 30, 187, 195, 226.

When reason serves God's revelation it does not judge it, rather it is judged by it. James puts it this way: 'But if you judge the law, you are not a doer of the law but a judge. There is only one lawgiver and judge, who is able to save and to destroy' (James 4:11, 12). Please note that ministerial reason is still reason, and not a leap in the dark. The great Genevan/Italian Reformed theologian François Turretini (1623–87) puts it this way, 'A ministerial and organic relation is quite different from a principal and despotic. Reason holds the former relation to theology, not the latter.' He adds that the right use of reason is to compare our propositions to the sacred Scripture, for 'reason itself neither can nor ought to be constituted the rule of belief.'[1]

What are the practical consequences of this distinction? The first and most obvious is this: when it can be determined that there is a true contradiction between the claims of the Bible and, say, the claims of philosophy, psychology, or science, we will have to align with Scripture, and wait for a possible reconciliation. Take, for example, the 'pop psychology' dictum that I must develop a good self-image. What is often meant by this is that I should feel good about myself, even when things don't go my way. The Bible acknowledges the dignity of all persons made after God's image, but it does not draw from that the conclusion that I should always feel good about myself. Indeed, there may be good reasons *not* to feel good about myself. The Bible wants

---

[1] Francis Turretin, *Institutes of Elenctic Theology*, ed. James Dennison, tr. George M. Giger, Vol. I (Phillipsburg: P & R Publishing, 1992–97), p. 25.

me to have a realistic self-image, one that acknowledges my sinfulness, my finitude, the world's brokenness, as well as my dignity. Ministerial reason looks to adjust both the question and the answer to biblical standards. This is true for many of our human opinions.

The second practical consequence is this: our thinking may benefit greatly from the various laws of logic proposed by the ancients and by such moderns as Irving Copi.[1] Bearing in mind that these laws of logic have their limitations, and are fallible, they can nevertheless help us as far as they go.

Perhaps the most universally acknowledged logical rule is the law of non-contradiction. Put in its simplest form, it teaches us that a statement cannot be true and not true at the same time and in the same way. Thus, when the Bible affirms that God is good, there can be no way in which he is also not good. So when Habakkuk declares, 'You … are of purer eyes than to see evil and cannot look at wrong' (Hab. 1:13), or when James affirms that God is 'the Father of lights with whom there is no variation or shadow due to change' (James 1:17), there is no room for anything opposite. What, then, do we make of passages in the Bible which tell us, for example, that God sent an evil spirit on Saul (1 Sam. 19:9), or when God says, 'I make well-being and create calamity' ('create evil' KJV; Isa. 45:7)? The law of non-contradiction forbids us to say that God is both good and evil. What we

---

[1] Irving M. Copi, with Carl Cohen & Kenneth D. McMahon, *Introduction to Logic*, 14th edition (Boston: Routledge, 2016).

need to do here is to examine whether a good God can nevertheless send judgments on rebellious people. Does sending an evil spirit make him complicit with evil? No, because once evil is in the world he can use it for his own good purposes. The ultimate example of this is the cross of Christ, which was both an act of lawlessness by wicked men and yet an event that was planned by God (Acts 2:23).

A ministerial use of the law of non-contradiction will also help us deal with apparent contradictions. For example, can God be utterly sovereign while, at the same time, human beings can make significant choices and decisions for which they are responsible? Or think of the claim of the so-called 'open theists' who teach that a fully sovereign God cannot really be compassionate, for if he controls all things why do evil things happen to good people? How can God be sovereign and compassionate at the same time? He must surely be one or the other. This is where another logical principle can help us, for it enables us put the law of non-contradiction into perspective. It is the principle known as *reductio ad absurdum*, which will alert us to the danger of taking one truth and pushing it to an absurd extreme. When the Protestant Reformers proclaimed justification by faith alone, they were strongly opposed by those who had a concern for the propriety of good works. They took the reformers' doctrine of justification and reduced it in such as way a to make the absurd claim that one cannot have both a free gift of righteousness and a responsibility for obedience. Another example of *reduction* is the so-called 'slippery slope' argument, an example of which could be,

'If you let your children watch movies, then the next thing you know, they will abandon Christian ethics.'

The ministerial use of reason is a large field. It is worth learning the field and cultivating the proper discipline it requires. The Bible encourages us to think soundly, with the proper use of logic, about the issues before us. 'Good sense ['good understanding' kjv] wins favour' (Prov. 13:15). Paul prays that the Lord may give the Ephesians 'a spirit of wisdom and of revelation in the knowledge of him' (Eph. 1:17). May it be so of us as we grow in his grace.

9

Reading the Bible: Illumination

*And we have something more sure, the prophetic word,
to which you will do well to pay attention as to a lamp
shining in a dark place, until the day dawns and the
morning star rises in your hearts.*

—The Apostle Peter

Neither our faith nor our reason are the *sources* of
our knowledge. They are the *organs* of knowledge.
The source must ultimately be God himself, by the inner
testimony of the Holy Spirit. The word of God is objective.
We read it with our natural capacities. But if we are going
to really hear the word of God rightly, if we are going to
interpret it correctly and be moved by it, our ultimate
internal principle will need the Holy Spirit's illumination.
To be sure, I am the one doing the believing, not the Holy
Spirit believing for me. That would make no sense. Yet,
only when God reveals himself to me, illuminating my
understanding, will I then be able to say, 'Jesus is Lord'
(1 Cor. 12:3).

A Dangerous God

Revelation is not first of all a cosy idea. 'God is love,' of course (1 John 4:8), but that should not obscure the fact that he is 'a consuming fire' (Heb. 12:29). In his endearing autobiography, *Surprised by Joy*, British writer C. S. Lewis (1898–1963) discusses the dreadfulness of divine revelation: 'People who are naturally religious find difficulty in understanding the horror of such a revelation. Amiable agnostics will talk cheerfully about "man's search for God". To me, as I then was, they might as well have talked about the mouse's search for the cat.'[1] There is a once popular Victorian poem entitled *The Hound of Heaven* in which the following lines describe God's unrelenting pursuit of unworthy creatures, only because he loves them.

> And human love needs human meriting:
>   How hast thou merited—
> Of all man's clotted clay the dingiest clot?
>   Alack, thou knowest not
> How little worthy of any love thou art!
> Who wilt thou find to love ignoble thee,
>   Save Me, save only Me?
> All which I took from thee I did but take
>   Not for thy harms,
> But just that thou might'st seek it in My arms.[2]

We use the term *special revelation* to differentiate it from *general revelation* (or what we can learn about God

[1] C. S. Lewis, *Surprised by Joy* (London, Glasgow: Collins Fontana, 1955), pp. 181-82.

[2] Francis Thompson, 'The Hound of Heaven,' *Poems* (New York: The Modern Library, 1893), pp. 88-93.

from creation). Whereas God is always being revealed in the natural world, in our conscience, and in history and culture, there are special interventions by which God manifests himself in remarkable ways to display his purposes. There are many books about special revelation in which his visitations are described.[1] Our concern here is rather with how our Christian minds may best understand and receive God's objective, powerful self-disclosures.

It is important to say at the outset that whereas there is great diversity in the events and the words that are considered special revelation, they are not disconnected or isolated, but are part of a single, organic whole, a system of witnesses that work together to achieve God's great redemptive purposes. However rich and diverse his deeds and his words, they all work together to contribute to the same purpose. And just as God is the author of the revelation, so is he its very content. Thus, there is one purpose to revelation: that people should discover how they may know, honour, serve, and glorify their creator and redeemer.

Special revelation is trinitarian. Thus, it does not simply divulge that there is one God and one plan of redemption, but that each person of the Trinity, Father, Son and Holy Spirit is involved. And though the persons are equal in their deity, and are of one mind in their intentions, they voluntarily took on different roles in the work of redemption. The Father is the originator of the plan of redemption,

---

[1] One of the best, and most accessible is Herman Bavinck, *Our Reasonable Faith: A Survey of Christian Doctrine*, tr. Henry Zylstra (Grand Rapids: Eerdmans, 1956), esp. pp. 61-115.

its administrator and overseer (Eph. 1:3-6). The Son is the accomplisher of salvation, being incarnate and going to Calvary, followed by his resurrection and ascension on our behalf (Eph. 1:7-12). The Holy Spirit applies the work of the Son to believers and makes salvation a present reality for them, equipping them for the new life they will lead (Eph. 1:13-14).

Nowhere is special revelation more clearly and more definitively set down than in the book we call the Bible. The Bible is the divinely inspired covenant book. The word 'inspired' is perhaps misleading. We speak of an inspired speech or of an inspired poem, meaning they were stirring or rousing. The ancient Greeks talked of the role of the Muse in guiding their music or their philosophy. The biblical idea of inspiration is quite different, stronger, more directly the product of God's initiative than the activity of a Muse. A classic expression of the biblical view is affirmed by the apostle Paul in his second letter to Timothy: 'All Scripture is breathed out by God and profitable for teaching, for reproof, for correction, and for training in righteousness, that the man of God may be competent, equipped for every good work' (2 Tim. 3:16). The Greek word translated 'breathed out' is *theopneustos*, a special construction meaning something like God-breathed. The reference is not to the authors, or to their inspired state. The reference is to the product, the entirety of the Scriptures. In the Old Testament, the breath of God, or the Spirit of God, is the very emanation, the outflowing or pouring forth of his power and renewing grace.

Thus, we may boldly state that the words of the Bible are God's own words. Throughout both Old and New Testaments, what the prophets and apostles said was identified with God's own speech (1 Kings 22:8-16; Psa. 119; Rom. 3:2; 1 Cor. 6:16; Heb. 3:7; 2 Pet. 1:20). This doesn't mean that the Bible was mechanically dictated, or that the personalities or concerns of the human authors counted for naught. We can identify the careful historical concerns of Luke (Luke 1:1-4), or the evangelistic aspiration of John (John 20:30-31). Consider the powerful imagery used by the psalmists or the author of Proverbs. The language of the different biblical authors is often a clue to their concerns, or to the cultural characteristics of their times, ones that influenced the way they articulated certain thoughts. So while appreciating that God did not mechanically dictate the contents of Scripture but used many different human authors, nevertheless we can say that the ultimate authority of every portion of the Bible bears the divine authority of the trinitarian God.

The Inspiration for Saving Knowledge

If we are to grasp these matters, we will need divine assistance. Dangers abound here.

The first is, armed with the claim of the Spirit's illumination, we think we possess an authority higher than others. This is not how illumination works. Some Christians all too casually will say, 'The Lord told me this' or 'God told me that.' Without denying the reality at times of the promptings of the Holy Spirit, nothing authorizes us to claim an authority higher than the Bible's. We can so easily slouch into subjectivism. The Bible is meant to be our sufficient resource for guidance and wisdom. Consider the proper preposition here: the testimony of the Holy Spirit is not along *with* Scripture, but *to* the Scripture.

A second danger is rationalism. If we only see the Bible as a repository of doctrines or propositions, and assume that when we have rummaged them out we are somehow blessed by the Spirit, then we have missed the active role of faith. When the sacred book is before us, we need to be able to pray for divine wisdom to the One who gives it generously (James 1:16-18; 4:5-8; 1 Cor. 4:7). The Bible is not a dictionary, but a covenant book requiring our allegiance. Prayer is a principal *entrée* into the riches of God's word.

A third danger is to trust unthinkingly in the authority of the church. This tends to be the position of the Roman Catholic faith. It is based on the idea that Jesus promised Peter he would build his church on his authority as the first pope. But the account in Matthew of Peter's confession, followed by the promise that the keys of the kingdom would be given to him, is not a justification for the papacy but of the authority of a confessing apostolic church (Matt. 16:18-19). It is true that the church is the 'pillar and ground of the truth,' and that much has been entrusted to her (1 Tim. 3:15), but her authority is only as valid as her faithfulness to Scripture. The Protestant Reformation established the principle, at great cost to itself, that church councils could and did err.

A fourth danger, the greatest of all, is to deny the finality of revelation in Jesus Christ. Many of the cults will say something like this: the Bible is fine, but here is one more book which you will need, or one more voice you should heed, if you are going to understand the Bible properly. This is the position of Islam, which says, Jewish and Christian religions were fine, but now they are in need of correction by the prophet Muhammad. Mormonism says the same about the utterances of Joseph Smith. The problem is that in God's economy everything that matters has indeed been accomplished! Only one more event is necessary to complete the entire plan of redemption, and that is the judgment (Heb. 9:27-28). There is nothing in between. Certainly, there is much to learn, but always from what has already been revealed (Heb. 2:1-4). Jesus warned us not to listen to false voices proclaiming, 'lo he is here, lo, he is there' (Matt. 24:23; Mark 13:21; Luke 17:23). We have Jesus and the completed Bible!

Bible Basics

How may our minds best grasp the true meaning of Scripture? How will the Spirit of God illumine us to understand God's word?

(1) The first principle is to remember that it is indeed the word of God, and thus to read it submissively and expectantly. When we read it, we should expect to meet with God himself. Not all of the Bible introduces us to God in equally obvious ways. But all of it does. Thus, there may be laws, or genealogies, or even poetic texts that appear to us secondary to the main message of Scripture. But they really are not. They are necessary parts of the whole. Some

parts of the Bible bristle with lucidity and brilliance. This is why many college workers start with the Gospel of John or Mark with their students. Other parts, though less immediately prominent, repay patient reading and study. Have a look at the pages of your closed Bible. Where are they dark from use, and where are they light? Genesis, the Psalms, the Gospels and perhaps much of the New Testament are darker. But what about Kings and Chronicles? Or the book of Proverbs? Or the Minor Prophets? When Paul wrote that *all* Scripture is God-breathed, he really meant it!

(2) A second principle to bear in mind is the unity and diversity of the Bible. Here is a distinction suggested by Richard Bauckham that may be helpful. The Bible is a unified story, but not necessarily a single narrative.[1] The Bible presents a coherent account of the world, from the creation to the new creation. It does so through different *genres*, or types of writing. Some is indeed narrative, such as Kings and the Gospels. Other portions are prophetic, apocalyptic, legal, poetic, doctrinal, etc. The Bible does not contain a single narrative, the way an author might write a novel, or even an historian write an historical account. Still, every part contributes to the whole story, much the way different melodies form a unified symphony.

(3) A third principle for the mind to respect is the progressive unfolding of revelation. Everything of importance was not revealed all at once. The first people needed to

---

[1] Richard Bauckham, *The Bible in the Contemporary World* (Grand Rapids & Cambridge: Eerdmans, 2015), chapter 1.

engage in culture. Noah's children needed to rediscover the covenant. Abraham's descendants needed to know of God's faithfulness. There needed to be a law-giver, then kings in Israel. Finally, the ultimate revelation, where everything is fulfilled and finalized, is in Jesus Christ. Putting it starkly, John tells us, 'And from his fullness we have all received, grace upon grace. For the law was given through Moses, grace and truth came through Jesus Christ' (John 1:16-17). All the Bible is about Jesus Christ (Luke 24:25-27; John 5:39). But it reveals him through seasons of revelation, over many centuries and in many different modes.

(4) Fourth, because of the Bible's coherency there are no real contradictions. This is a point difficult for modern people to accept. But if the Scripture is really the word of God, how could God contradict himself or mislead his people? This does not mean there are no difficulties in the Bible. There are even apparent contradictions. Some are in the narratives. In one account Judas hanged himself (Matt 27:5). In another he fell and burst open (Acts 1:18). There are ways to reconcile these two versions. Perhaps he stayed hanged for a long time until his body decayed. It may be best not to worry about such things! Others might be of greater concern. For example, Paul tells us in the same sentence to work out our own salvation and that it is God who is at work in us (Phil. 2:12-13). We are tempted to ask, well, which is it? But this sort of paradox teaches us something of the mystery of God's ways. Our efforts are not only not opposed to God's, but they are energized by his. Some apparent contradictions are in the ways the

narrators select their materials. First and Second Kings emphasize Israel's decline into immorality. First and Second Chronicles emphasize God's faithfulness despite Israel's degeneration. Both are true, and each author purposed to stress one truth which complements the other. Perhaps the greatest requirement here is humility. While good scholars can help us resolve many of the tensions we think we see, no one has all the answers. That is as it should be, since God alone is ultimate.

Think on These Things

Since the Bible is not a textbook, nor is it a dictionary, it is appropriate that we study it in a special way. Many methods can be adduced. There are countless guides to reading the Bible. Some bring you through the entire book in a year. Some concentrate on individual texts. Devotional books abound. Many of them are good and edifying. Of course, this is where we put our minds to work. Here is a call to study the Scripture, to examine it closely, to compare passage with passage. We have been given many tools for this purpose, such as pastors, commentaries, Bible dictionaries and the like. I have found it best to hold off using these tools before I have personally confronted the texts and drawn my own conclusions. Prayer is the necessary companion to Bible reading. Since it is God's word, we should feel no compunction in asking him to illumine our understanding.

The Bible invites us not only to know its propositions but to absorb its wisdom. The fountain of all wisdom is Jesus

Christ. He is called 'the power of God and the wisdom of God' (1 Cor. 1:24). Paul prays that the Father of glory may give us the Spirit of wisdom (Eph. 1:17). He pleads for the word of Christ to dwell in us richly, as we teach one another in all wisdom (Col. 3:16). What is this wisdom, so prized by the apostle? It is the knowledge God possesses, the insight by which he thinks and through which he has made the world (Prov. 3:19; 8:22). The book of Proverbs is an anthology of wise sayings which are meant to guide us in life. Wisdom is not something you *get* once and for all. It is a lifelong set of skills that make you strong and resolute.

One skill I believe is underdeveloped is that of *meditation*. Christian meditation is full of content. It does not join you to the cosmos but it can bring you closer to the God who made it. The opening psalm in the Psalter tells us that the believer not only delights in the law of the Lord but 'meditates' on it day and night (Psa. 1:2). Psalm 119 is the perfect example of such meditation on the word of God. It not only teaches us to meditate but guides us in that practice. 'I will meditate on your precepts and fix my eyes on your ways,' it tells us (Psa. 119:15). Indeed, the entire psalm is a free-flowing reflection on God's word. It is an acrostic poem, wherein every section is composed of eight verses beginning with the same letter of the Hebrew alphabet. This kind of structure is used by the poet to look at different aspects of God's word, as we might look at different facets of a mobile.[1]

---

[1] A work of art, usually hung from the ceiling, with various moving parts. The twentieth-century mobile master was Alexander Calder.

Memorization is a lost art too. Interestingly the Hebrew word for meditation in Psalm 1 is something like 'to mutter.' It is used of doves that 'chatter' (Isa. 31:4; 59:11). The psalmist mouthed the words of Scripture day and night, and so should we. Memorization should not be mindless, but full of thought. Charles Spurgeon puts it unforgettably:

> Oh, that you and I might get into the very heart of the word of God, and get that word into ourselves! As I have seen the silkworm eat into the leaf, and consume it, so ought we to do with the word of the Lord—not crawl over its surface, but eat right into it till we have taken it into our inmost parts.[1]

The apostle Paul exhorted the Colossian believers to 'let the word of Christ dwell in you richly' (Col. 3:16). We have looked briefly at some of the means to accomplish that. Let us, then, read the word regularly, study it patiently, meditate on it thoughtfully, memorize it religiously, and above all, in dependence on God, praying that he would shine into our hearts to give us the light of the knowledge of his glory in the face of Jesus Christ (2 Cor. 4:6).

---

[1] From *The Autobiography of Charles H. Spurgeon, Compiled from His Letters, Diaries, and Records by His Wife and Private Secretary, Vol. IV, 1878-1892* (London: Curtis & Jennings, 1900), p. 268.

10

Worldview and Calling

The point is that throughout history Christians have found it a missiological imperative to explain to non-believers the coherence of the biblical message and to relate it in a logical and coherent way to the culture of their day. Proof texting is simply inadequate in this respect.

—Craig Bartholomew

The Christian faith is not simply a set of individual doctrines. It is not piecemeal. It is certainly not just a moral system or a set of rules. It is a coherent philosophy of life. One of the unfortunate characteristics of much modern Christian faith is that it is *dualistic*. That is, the world is split into two components, a heavenly realm and an earthly realm. The most important matters are 'spiritual,' that is, they pertain to prayer, worship, Bible study, the sacraments, and missions. The rest of life is a necessity, but is of secondary importance. Such things as political involvement, artistic endeavours, scientific research, the practice of law, while inevitable, are at best in a supporting role. Critics of Christian cultural involvement like to quote 1950s radio preacher J. Vernon McGee, who asked the rhetorical question, 'Do you polish brass on a sinking ship?' He was apparently referring to the decline of civilization, and thus warning Christians against any kind of investment in the things of this world. The only kind of activity worth pursuing is 'soul-winning.'

This view is fraught with problems. The first is that there can be no alternative to the question the way it is posed. It's rather like being asked, 'When did you stop beating your wife?' The assumption that all of civilization is but a sinking ship needs serious examination. And what if the ship were worth saving? Not polishing the brass, but perhaps repairing the hull would be in order.[1] Even if the comparison of the world to a ship has some merit, suggesting all cultural engagement is like polishing brass shows little understanding of how a ship actually functions. And even if the world is sinking like a ship, the lack of love for a world that God made, albeit now fallen, is contrary to the gospel, wherein God so loved the world that he sacrificed his Son in order to save it. How ironic that God did save an entire civilization through a large ship in the days of Noah![2] Certainly, the priority of doing evangelism in relation to cultural pursuits is a legitimate one. The Christian mind

[1] This point is made by Joel McDurmon, 'Do You Polish the Brass on a Sinking Ship?' See https://americanvision.org/3596/do-you-polish-the-brass-on-a-sinking-ship/#footnote_0_3596.

[2] Joel McDurmon, 'Do You Polish the Brass?'

must address those priorities. But at the very least, we are told to care for the poor, to pray for governing authorities, to hold marriage in honour, to work diligently. These are not luxuries but part of the work of God's kingdom.

The Character of Calling

A dualistic view of life has a long pedigree. Consider Eusebius, bishop of Caesarea (d. 339). In his *Demonstration of the Gospel* he answers various questions about the Bible and the Christian life. At one point he declares that 'the church of Christ has two kinds of lifestyle.' The first is the 'perfect life,' and the second is the 'permitted life.' To the first belong priests, monks and religious women. To the second belong all others, such as farmers, traders, or family members.[1] Many centuries later, the priest Thomas à Kempis (1380–1471) says something similar in *The Imitation of Christ*, which became a classic of Christian devotion. While containing many helpful directives for practising spiritual life, the larger premise upon which its four books stand is questionable. The full title of the first book is *The Imitation of Christ and Contempt for the Vanities of the World.*[2] The first book encourages us to renounce all that is vain and illusory, including proud learning. But it does

[1] Eusebius of Caesarea, 'To Marinus,' in *Gospel Problems and Solutions*, ed. Roger Pearce, tr. David J. D. Miller (Ipswich: Chieftain Publishing, 2010). See also the summary of Eusebius in the marvellous book by Os Guinness, *The Call: Finding and Fulfilling the Central Purpose of Your Life* (Nashville: Word, 1998), pp. 32-33.

[2] Many editions exist. One of the best is *The Imitation of Christ*, ed. Joseph N. Tylenda (New York: Vintage, 1998).

not tell us about the good things of creation, including God-glorifying learning. The second book tells us when persecuted to bear our cross willingly, not grudgingly. But it does not tell us how to live in God's world when we are not being persecuted. The third book tells us to leave ourselves behind and desire nothing outside of ourselves. But it says nothing of the plethora of legitimate desires. The final book encourages us to receive the Eucharist (Lord's Supper) by cleansing our hearts. That is indisputable, except that the emphasis on the sacrament conveys the idea that church life and ritual are worth more than any other activity.

The net effect of the ancient view was to divide God's people according to two purposes. The first are the called ones. They have a vocation, which could be holy orders, missions, theologians, or the like. Everyone else is obliged to live in the world outside of vocation, and if possible to support the called ones. We might refer to this as the sacred/secular dichotomy. These outsiders might even benefit from the sacred realm by coming to mass, going on pilgrimage, supporting the church, etc., but they lived in the secular realm. This view is still found today. We speak of a 'crisis of vocations,' meaning a decline in ministers. Modern Christians might speak of someone being called to the mission field.

The Reformation of the sixteenth century blew this dualism apart. Martin Luther, mentioned earlier, challenged this dichotomy in a number of works. One was *The Babylonian Captivity of the Church* (1520). The treatise was a 'deadly dagger aimed at the very heart of sacramentalism and clericalism and monasticism.'[1] Radically enough, Luther recommended abolishing all vows, whether for entering a religious order or for going on pilgrimage, or any other resolution. One's baptismal vows were quite enough. Buried with his argument is a revolutionary sentence: 'the works of monks and priests, however holy and arduous they may be, do not differ one whit in the sight of God from the works of the rustic labourer in the field or the woman going about her household tasks, but that all works are measured before God by faith alone.'[2] He goes on to add his views on marriage, and pleads that it be 'deregulated' so that it could be enjoyed by a great many.[3] Finally, he decries the 'detestable tyranny' of the clergy over the laity and reminds the reader that every baptized Christian is a priest (1 Pet. 2:9).[4]

This ground-breaking view grew and matured in the other reformers and then in the Puritans. But it opened the door for an understanding of the Christian faith as a worldview, not an elite calling to a higher realm. Perhaps no one developed worldview thinking more deeply that Abraham Kuyper (1837–1920) the Dutch theologian, scholar, and statesman. In his remarkable *Lectures on Calvinism* (1898) he developed the idea that the Christian faith was a 'life-system,' or a 'life-and-worldview.'[5] It is of interest

---

[1] 'Introduction' in Martin Luther, *The Babylonian Captivity of the Church*, tr. A. T. W. Steinhäuser (Philadelphia: Fortress Press, 1959), p. 119.

[2] Martin Luther, *Babylonian Captivity*, pp. 202-3.

[3] Martin Luther, *Babylonian Captivity*, pp. 220-37.

[4] Martin Luther, *Babylonian Captivity*, p. 244.

[5] Abraham Kuyper, *Lectures on Calvinism*, 8th edition (Grand Rapids: Eerdmans, 1987).

that his burden to see the Christian faith in this way was for the purpose of opposing it to the prevailing worldview of modernity. The turning point giving modernism its contemporary power was the French Revolution (1789). Although there were certain legitimate causes to this upheaval, its basic *principle* was a profound anti-Christian cancer.[1]

What conditions needed to be met in order to oppose modernism with the Christian worldview? Three of them: (1) our relationship to God, (2) our relationship to human-kind, and (3) our relationship to the world.[2] To be fully Christian, a worldview must originate in the regenerate heart that lives before God. As such, our worldview will have to be nurtured in prayer and illuminated by the Holy Spirit. Kuyper once remarked, 'Stress in creedal confession, without drinking these waters [of the soul's nearness to God], runs dry in barren orthodoxy, just as truly spiritual emotion, without clearness in confessional standards, makes one sink in the bog of sickly mysticism.'[3]

If we are tempted to think worldview is extraneous, consider the implications of the Lord's Prayer.[4] Seen one

[1] Abraham Kuyper, *Lectures on Calvinism*, pp. 2-3.

[2] For a clear presentation of the way worldview relates to God, human-ity and the world in Kuyper, see Craig G. Bartholomew, *Contours of the Kuyperian Tradition: A Systematic Introduction* (Downers Grove: IVP Academic, 2017), pp. 108-14.

[3] See Abraham Kuyper, *To Be Near Unto God* (New York: Macmillan, revised edition, 1925), p. 6.

[4] A few years ago I wrote a book called *A Transforming Vision: The Lord's Prayer as a Lens for Life* (Fearn, Ross-shire: Christian Focus Publications, 2014), in which I argued this point.

way, that prayer really contains a worldview. *Our Father, who art in heaven*: all centres on the infinite and personal God of the universe. *Hallowed be thy name*: this God is due all worship and all allegiance. *Thy kingdom come*: God has called us to his central purpose, advancing his reign and his righteousness over all the earth. *Thy will be done, on earth as it is in heaven*: in this broken world, God's will is not yet fully accomplished. *Give us this day our daily bread*: God provides everything we need, if we are willing to wait for his timing. *And forgive us our debts as we forgive our debtors*: we are miserable sinners in need of God's forgiveness. *And lead us not into temptation, but deliver us from evil*: only if the Lord spares us from trials too hard to bear may we hope to complete our journey to heaven. *For thine is the kingdom and the power and the glory, forever, Amen*: 'For from him and through him and to him are all things. To him be the glory forever. Amen' (Rom. 11:36).

11

Worldview Thinking

It is not only that true spirituality covers all of life,
but it covers all parts of the spectrum of life equally.
In that sense there is nothing concerning reality that
is not spiritual.

—Francis A. Schaeffer

Not everyone is comfortable thinking that the Christian faith is a worldview. Some objections are plausible. It is only recently that the term has come into popular use. We are still perhaps adjusting to its usefulness, and its insufficiencies. Here we will look at a few of the possible challenges to the notion of worldview and attempt to provide some helpful answers.

The Extent of Worldview

Some people fear worldview's putative imperialism. Is there a Christian view of absolutely everything? We can answer that question in a number of ways. If we are asking what the Bible has to say about nuclear disarmament or about setting the speed limit on a motorway, of course the answer is negative. But this answer must immediately be nuanced. First, the Bible is not a textbook. Indeed, when we understand the kind of book it is, we will realize it does not have specific legislation for most of what we need to know in life. Even in areas which we might think are quite thoroughly treated in Scripture, we realize it is not a rule book. Consider marriage, for example. The Bible has a good deal to say about marriage: when to enter into it, the requirement for couples to remain faithful, holding the institution in honour, the propriety of having children, and the like. But it does not tell us whom to marry, what faithfulness looks like in detail, the social standing of marriage compared to other institutions, how many children to have, and other specifics. The Bible highly commends marriage, since it is instated at the creation, and since Jesus honoured it by performing his first miracle at a wedding feast. It tells us marriage is monogamous, heterosexual, and for life. But so many aspects of marriage are left up to the wisdom of the couple: where to live, what career to pursue, how often to have family worship, where to attend church, what kind of school to send the children to, and so forth.

Second, therefore, when we respect the way Scripture speaks of life, it in fact does tell us something about everything. The same God who knows all things and who has answers for all things has chosen to reveal some of them in the Bible and some of them by implication, or, as the framers of the *Westminster Confession of Faith* put it, 'by good and necessary consequence' (1.6). Although nuclear weapons did not exist in biblical times, the Bible has a good deal to say about armed defence. We may legitimately derive principles from Scripture about when to go to war and how to conduct it when in combat. An important part of our deriving such principles requires us to respect the different seasons of revelation. And so, for example, we would not simply conclude from Joshua's conquest that our every military endeavour will be blessed by God. The occupation of Canaan by the people of Israel was a unique episode in human history. It led to the theocracy, wherein Israel's life was meant to be a model for the final judgment and the inauguration of the new heavens and the new earth. When Israel failed to remain faithful, God's people were sent into exile, and a new kingdom was installed, through Jesus Christ. The principles of justice are now extended to all people through the civil magistrate (Rom. 13:1-7). In our era, neither Joshua, nor the angel of the Lord, but the civil authority is God's servant, 'an avenger who carries out God's wrath on the wrongdoer' (Rom. 13:4).

The weapon of the Roman judicial officer was the sword. Jesus told his disciples to be peacemakers (Matt. 5:9). Paul tells his readers in Rome to live peaceably with all, if possible (Rom. 12:18). The presumption is of making great efforts to avoid warfare unless it becomes a sad necessity. Our modern judicial officers have in hand far more destructive weaponry than the sword. One of the most terrifying is the nuclear bomb. The question is, does the same principle of peacemaking until proven impossible apply today, or are there certain kinds of warfare that are by their nature immoral? I believe the principles are the same, though one would want a nuclear option to be the very, very last resort.[1] Nuclear disarmament is the ideal, and yet realism would require us to keep certain options open.

The point here is not to settle the complex question of nuclear disarmament, but to argue for the relevance of Scripture for every issue, including ones that could not have been precisely foreseen by its authors. The same applies to setting speed limits, and other traffic regulations. So in this sense our biblical worldview is about everything.

Defending the Centre

It is possible to get caught-up in minutiae, and to apply the Christian faith with great certainty to areas of life that are at best secondary, not to say unimportant. A few cautions are in order. First, it is crucial to distinguish between the centre of our worldview and the periphery. The centre of our worldview is the tri-personal God. He is the origin of all things. He created the world upright and gave his creation the imprimatur of his character. But we have transgressed that beautiful original order, and as a consequence we are sinful and the world in which we live is broken. Yet God has not left us to our own devices, but has devised a plan for the redemption of his people through the death and resurrection of his son, Jesus Christ. This centre is sometimes summarized by the triad, *creation–fall–redemption*. Other summaries may be at least as useful. The Apostles' Creed is

[1] The *jus ad bellum* is not as straightforward as it might appear. See Michael Waltzer, *Just and Unjust Wars: A Moral Argument with Historical Illustrations* (New York: Basic Books, 2015).

a particularly compelling one. As we move from this centre to the outside, we still try to be faithful to Scripture. But like nuclear disarmament or speed limits on the motorway, there is a greater margin for variation.

As we move outward from the centre to the periphery we should exercise great caution to be sure we can relate more marginal issues to the centre. There is undoubtedly a Christian view of fashion, or of board games, or of bookbinding, but those kinds of issues should be approached with a very light hand.

Another, related critique of worldview thinking is what people perceive to be its rationalism: everything in its place, with no room for wisdom or worship. Worldview often comes across as purely cognitive, with no place for the full range of human faculties. That might be fair enough in some cases. Defenders of worldview thinking, Richard Middleton and Brian Walsh, told us worldview thinking answers four question: Where am I? Who am I? What's wrong? What's the remedy?[1] These are helpful as far as they go. What we do not see, though surely the authors believe it, is the rich array of social, expressive, and spiritual aspects stemming from the heart-commitment at the foundation of the worldview. The development of a worldview is much more than merely cognitive answers to four questions. It is a spiritual endeavour. We hold to our worldview as we hold to the object of our worship. In the case of the gospel

---

[1] Brian J. Walsh & Richard J. Middleton, *The Transforming Vision: Shaping a Christian Worldview* (Downers Grove: InterVarsity Press, 1984), p. 35.

we align our worldview with the worship of the triune God. In the case of unbelief our worldview grows out of our worship of the creature.

Yet another critique of worldview thinking is that it resembles a social programme. To be sure, some who hear the term 'worldview' may think it is a simplistic platform for social change, without taking account of the gospel's call to conversion. That would be tragic. It certainly has nothing to do with Abraham Kuyper's original idea, since he was profoundly convinced not only of the need for conversion, but for a daily walk with the Lord. At the other end of the spectrum, however, some would simply assume that the key to social change is to effect enough conversions so that social change would be the natural fruit. There is something to that. However, in most historical cases this process was at best incomplete. Both in Europe and in North America, the great revivals in the nineteenth century had some effect on the moral improvement of society.[1] Yet by the mid-century, 'the dream of a moral Christian society, transformed outwardly by the voluntary efforts of the inwardly converted, began to collapse.'[2] The problems of industrialization, and, in North America, the challenges of Native American rights and of slavery, proved too daunting.

One of the problems is that worldview thinking can be associated with a naïve 'transformationist' view of how to

[1] See Timothy L. Smith, *Revivalism and Social Reform* (Eugene, OR: Wipf & Stock, 2004).
[2] Mark Noll, *The Old Religion in a New World* (Grand Rapids: Eerdmans, 2004), p. 104.

engage in culture. Such a view can be triumphalist and also over-simple. Certainly there are structures and patterns we will want to interact with if we are to see change. But as Americans say, there is no silver bullet. That is, there is no one strategy that will lead to measurable change. Entering politics is sometimes believed to be the *key* to social improvement. If only we could enact a few laws reflecting Christian values we could see significant change. The political realm has its place under the lordship of Christ, but it is only one of many, including family, business, media, and so forth. Larger strategies, such as serving the city, the academy, the arts, must be enacted in order to hope for change. The Christian faith is not a coercive religion. Nor is it merely passive. Change occurs when God's people live as believers and reach out to every level of society with the compassion of their Lord.[1]

A final critique of worldview thinking is that it denigrates the unique place of the church. The New Testament places an extraordinary emphasis on the church of Jesus Christ. Three overlapping characteristics distinguish the church. (1) It is a worshipping body. When God's people gather, their first priority is to worship the Lord. As the writer of Hebrews puts it, we have come to Mount Zion and to the city of the living God: 'Therefore let us be grateful for receiving a kingdom that cannot be shaken, and thus let us offer to God acceptable worship, with reverence and awe'

---

[1] There is a most helpful portion on these issues in Timothy J. Keller, *Loving the City: Doing Balanced, Gospel-Centered Ministry in Your City*, section two (Grand Rapids: Zondervan, 2016), pp. 210-17.

(Heb. 12:22, 28). (2) The church exists for the edification of believers. Primarily through the word preached and taught we grow into greater and greater maturity in Christ (Eph. 2:19-22). (3) The church reaches out to the needy world. The body of Christ must not only look upward, but outward, bringing the saving knowledge of Christ to the destitute world.

A solid Christian worldview ought to promote the central role of the church, not denigrate it. The church ought to be the primary place to nurture our worldview, to give it a proper theological orientation. What that should not mean is that the church must order all of life directly. The biblical worldview recognizes other social entities, such as the family, the school, government, business, the arts, and many others, as legitimate spheres over which Christ is Lord. The church cannot and must not do all of the work of kingdom extension. While the church is the guardian of God's word, it is not a centre of power which rules over the other sectors of society. It may be that through excitement about worldview thinking some Christians have neglected the church. But it also may be that through enthusiasm about the church some Christians have neglected the call to other spheres of endeavour.

12

Doing Science

I was merely thinking God's thoughts after him. Since
we astronomers are priests of the highest God in regard
to the book of nature, it benefits us to be thoughtful,
not of the glory of our minds, but rather, above all else,
of the glory of God.

—Johannes Kepler

The application of the Christian worldview is various. So many areas of life, indeed, ultimately, all of them can be illumined by our Christian worldview. Perhaps the first that comes to many minds is science.

The Book of Nature

It may not be the best of metaphors, but at least from the Middle Ages on, Christian thinkers have referred to the two great texts of God's self-disclosure, the Book of God (the Scriptures) and the Book of Nature (the Creation). William Shakespeare has the soothsayer in *Anthony and Cleopatra* say, 'In nature's infinite book of secrecy, a little I can read.' The twelfth-century sage Hugh of St Victor said,

'For this whole visible world is a book written by the finger of God.' He went on to say that 'just as some illiterate man who sees an open book looks at the figures but does not recognize the letters: just so the foolish natural man who does not perceive the things of God sees outwardly in these visible creatures the appearances but does not inwardly understand the reason.'[1]

There is no reason to limit God's fingerprint to the visible world. Though much harder to perceive, there is also an invisible world designed by God. Everything in the creation, visible, invisible, high above, low beneath, makes up God's creation. What we tend to call the universe, the Bible often refers to as the heavens and the earth (Gen. 1:1; 2:1, 4; see Psa. 50:4; 89:11; Isa. 42:5; Zech. 12:1; Heb. 1:10). This universe made by God is not simply a collection of atoms and energy, but it has a character. That character is its relation to God. The prophet calls for the heavens and the earth to sing and be joyful (Isa. 49:13). They are proof that God is God (Neh. 9:6; Psa. 57:11). They will be judged, and will eventually be shaken and transformed into the new heavens and the new earth (Jer. 4:23, 28; 10:11; Hag. 2:6; 2 Pet. 3:10, 13).

Every component of the creation teaches us something. The heavens are telling the glory of God, as we have mentioned (Psa. 19:1-2). God's voice is heard in the great waters (Psa. 29:3; Ezek. 1:24; 43:2; Rev. 1:15; 14:2). God's voice breaks

---

[1] Quoted in C. S. Singleton, *Commedia: Elements of Structure* (Cambridge, MA: Harvard University Press, 1965), p. 25.

the cedar trees (Psa. 29:5; Judg. 9:15). Light is God's garment, the clouds his chariot (Psa. 104:2, 3). God stretches out the heavens as a tent to dwell in (Isa. 40:22). He causes the seasons, the rain, the sunshine (Gen. 1:14; 8:22; Jer. 5:24; Matt. 5:45; Acts 14:17). When the harvest is abundant, it is not by chance, but by the goodness of the Lord, for he is the Lord of the harvest (Gen. 41:25-36; Matt. 9:38). All of these come from the Father's hand, by way of his covenant with all creatures (Gen. 9:15). Our Lord constantly referred to the creation in his teaching: 'A sower went out to sow' (Matt. 13:3); 'A man planted a vineyard' (Mark 12:1); 'He is like a man building a house' (Luke 6:48); 'No one after lighting a lamp covers it with a jar' (Luke 8:16); 'I am the door of the sheep' (John 10:7); 'I am the true vine' (John 15:1). Paul likens the resurrection to a seed sown in dishonour and raised in glory (1 Cor. 15:42-44).

The Origins of Modern Science

Today, many people will tell you there is a pitched battle between so-called religion and science. Usually, this view calls attention to the most prominent conflicts pitting scientific progress against the church. For example, Galileo was put under house arrest by the Inquisition for defending Copernicus' sun-centred planetary system. Or, another example, the Scopes trial of 1925 is cited, where a substitute teacher was accused of teaching human evolution, in violation of the laws of Tennessee. In an attempt to avoid the impression that there is a conflict, some have argued for NOMA, or non-overlapping magisteria. According to this model, science and religion have nothing to do with one another, since they address different realms: science examines the phenomena of the world, religion teaches spirituality and moral comportment, without claiming to touch upon the processes that explain the physical world. Of course, this approach is attractive, but in the end unsatisfactory, since the Bible is rooted in history and is not simply a guide to spirituality.

NOMA would have surprised the founders of modern science, since they considered the Christian faith to be one of the major factors in their explorations leading to the birth of modern science. From the Middle Ages to the Renaissance and Reformation there was a growing sense of man's authorization to explore the creation simply because God had made it. Admittedly it took the Christian church a number of centuries to read the book of nature less through the lens of Greek philosophy and more through the spectacles of Scripture. From our hindsight it is easy to reproach the church for being less than critical of the surrounding Greek and Roman culture into which she was born. The cosmologies of Plato and Aristotle were so pervasive that the more natural posture was to see how much Christian theology could work with them. Eventually, those cosmologies were displaced by a more biblical way of thinking.

The eminent astronomers Johannes Kepler (1571–1630) and Galileo Galilei (1564–1642) were Christians. They are considered among the chief architects of modern science. They boldly mounted a thoughtful criticism of Greek philosophy. The story is involved, though fascinating.[1] In contrast to Plato, both Kepler and Galileo believed in testing things empirically. One incident is telling. Most philosophers and theologians up until them believed that all the movements in the heavens were perfectly uniform and circular. But then Kepler carefully observed the planet Mars in its orbit, and found that there was a difference of eight minutes between the reality and the theoretical pattern everyone had believed. He declared, 'These eight minutes paved the way for the reformation of the whole of astronomy.'[2] Kepler was a Lutheran who believed God had made the world with a certain order, but not necessarily the order proclaimed by Aristotle. His courage to examine the world as it was paved the way to the scientific method.

Galileo's life was plagued by misadventures. But his stated goal was to prove the harmony between the two books, the book of nature and the book of Scripture. Like Kepler, he believed there ought to be corroboration for scientific theories from empirical measurement. Again, he

[1] Many accounts of the Christian influence on the birth of modern science exist. See *Puritanism and the Rise of Modern Science: The Merton Thesis*, ed. Bernard I. Cohen (New Brunswick, NJ: Rutgers University Press, 1990); John Hedley Brooke, *Science and Religion: Some Historical Perspectives* (Cambridge: Cambridge University Press, 1991); Peter Harrison, *The Bible, Protestantism, and the Rise of Natural Science* (Cambridge: Cambridge University Press, 1998); Ian G. Barbour, *Religion and Science: Historical and Contemporary Issues* (San Francisco: HarperOne, 1997).

[2] This incident is recounted in R. Hooykaas, *Religion and the Rise of Modern Science* (Grand Rapids: Eerdmans, 1972), pp. 35-36. Kepler published his *New Astronomy* in 1609. Among other things he accused Plato of violating piety.

was up against the prevailing Greek philosophy, accepted by the church. According to Aristotle, heavier objects ought to fall faster than lighter ones. Galileo put this to the test, and found out that no matter how large or small the objects, they fell at the same rate. For this discovery he was kicked out of the University of Pisa, though he landed at the more progressive University of Padua. There he put together one of the first telescopes, and observed the moon and the planets. He discovered that the surface of the moon was not smooth, as had been supposed. And he found out Venus had phases, which indicated that it orbited the sun. His major conflict, however, was when he confirmed Copernicus' view that the sun, not the earth, was at the centre of the planetary system. For this he was put under discipline by the Inquisition. His punishment was mild, but the incident became embarrassing for the Roman Catholic Church. Galileo was convinced he had biblical and theological support for his views.[1] The church eventually came around.

Anti-Materialist Thinking

Culture wars are not a new development. Materialism was one of the challenges Christians had to face shortly after the Reformation. Thomas Hobbes (1588–1679) author of *Leviathan* (1651) held a mechanistic understanding of human beings and the necessity of a strong central government.

---

[1] In his *Letter to the Grand Duchess Christina* (1615) he appeals to Augustine and Thomas Aquinas for the particular biblical interpretations that make room for a heliocentric system.

Many were appalled by his views, and by his apparent rejection of revealed religion. Among his most prominent opponents was Robert Boyle (1627–91). He forged the way for our understanding of how heat works, how acid tears things apart, and how cohesion puts them back together again. Interestingly, Boyle accepted the contours of a mechanical world, where matter is real, but whose motion is ordered by divine providence. He rejected the need for some sort of intermediary, believing that God could order the parts of the universe directly, by his great wisdom.[1] One of the founders of modern science, Robert Boyle believed that the more we learn about the world, the more we will encounter the attributes of the creator God.

Isaac Newton's major opponent was René Descartes (1642–1727). Descartes' rationalism led him to theories of light and gravity that did not sufficiently allow room for divine providence. Newton, possibly the greatest scientist of all time, held complex theological views, including struggles with the full divinity of Jesus Christ. But he certainly believed, in opposition to the materialists, that God had created this world and given it the order it possesses. 'This most beautiful system of the sun, planets, and comets, could only proceed from the counsel and dominion of an intelligent Being,' he declared in his masterpiece, the *Principia Mathematics*, Book III (1687). He modified Boyle's view to focus on *forces*. The world of forces could

[1] See, J. E. McGuire, 'Boyle's Conception of Nature,' *Journal of the History of Ideas*, 33 (1972), p. 533.

be described mathematically. God was in direct control of the forces, and indeed would 'rewind' them from time to time in order to avoid a breakdown.

During the closing decades of the seventeenth century this combination of Christian convictions and scientific explorations was fully expressed by the Fellows of the Royal Society of London. They were mostly Protestants in the Anglican tradition, who exercised different professions: noblemen, medical doctors, deans of cathedral towns, etc. Established in the years after the English Civil War, then the Commonwealth, and finally the Restoration of the Monarchy, there was surely a political motivation behind their attempts to show the world as a stable place. Yet through these circumstances these remarkable scientists held the conviction that there was a God who had designed the universe. Perhaps the outstanding figure in the Royal Society was Robert Hooke (1635–1703). His book, *Micrographia* (1665) uncovered the marvellous unseen world of the tiniest parts of creation. He is credited with identifying the plant cell. He did this because he believed in the creator God.

Believers in a biblical view of the world have continued to be on the forefront of scientific studies, despite the false narrative of the so-called war between religion and science. Even the unfortunate Scopes trial is not as one-sided as it has been portrayed in the movies. Scopes was in fact convicted, although the conviction was overturned on a technicality. To be sure, there has been animosity. One thinks of Jerry Coyne's hostile (and most superficial) critique of 'religion' in books such as *Faith vs Fact: Why Science and Religion Are Incompatible*.[1] But this is to ignore the numerous believers who have been on the forefront of great discoveries. One thinks of Michael Faraday (1791–1867) and the theory of electrolysis. One thinks of Gregor Mendel (1822–82) the Augustinian abbot who preached regularly, and was the father of modern genetics. Arthur Compton (1892–1962) the Baptist deacon who won the Nobel Prize in physics.

Most recently Francis Collins (b. 1950) led the way to mapping every gene in the human DNA, which was completed in 2003. Some consider it the most significant scientific breakthrough in generations. Collins has also led in the fight against cystic fibrosis and Huntington's disease. He is a committed Christian who has written on the compatibility between science in general, genetics in particular, and the Christian faith.[2] And there are a host of others.

Two major motivations can be found for those who use their minds in the advancement of science. The first is to investigate the wonders of God's ways. The second is to combat the ill effects of the fall. Instead of the defeatism of many Christians who are convinced the battle for the truth in the realm of science has been lost, we need to be galvanized by the great biblical call to declare the glory of God in the created realm.

[1] New York: Penguin, 2016.
[2] Francis Collins, *The Language of God: A Scientist Presents Evidence for Belief* (New York: The Free Press, 2006).

13

The Moral Order

Culture may even be described simply as that which makes life worth living.—T. S. Eliot

While science may appear to be the principal playing field for the encounter of the Christian mind with the creation, there are many others. Theologian Herman Bavinck once remarked, 'Nature and history are the books of God's omnipotence and wisdom, his goodness and justice. All peoples have to a certain extent recognized this revelation.'[1]

History

First, a simple, but profound point. Biblical religion is rooted and grounded in history, as we saw earlier. God's redemptive work takes place in history. Today we are aware more than in times past of the progressive unfolding of revelation, and thus we have learned to read the Bible with the awareness of the successive seasons of God's

[1] J. H. Bavinck, *Reformed Dogmatics, Vol. I, Prolegomena*, p. 310.

redemptive work. The great biblical scholar Geerhardus Vos (1862–1949) describes the Bible as 'the history of special revelation.' He explains that redemption is not all at once, but historically successive, and so must be the revelation that accompanies it. This process is incarnate in history, culminating in Jesus Christ.[1]

Perhaps surprisingly, the full awareness of the historical dimension of human life was not manifest until the nineteenth century. It developed for a number of reasons. The Romantic movement featured a deeper sense of nationality, and a corresponding development of historical literature, as in the work of Sir Walter Scott (1771–1832) and Honoré de Balzac (1799–1850). By the twentieth century historian Johan Huizinga (1872–1945) could say, 'historical thinking has entered our very blood.'[2] Unfortunately, along with the strengths of the historical perspective came certain weaknesses. One of them is known as *historicism*, or the view that human, material historical forces explain everything about the human condition, leaving out divine providence as well as human freedom. Still, greater awareness of process, movement, development, these are good in themselves.

---

[1] Geerhardus Vos, *Biblical Theology* (Grand Rapids: Eerdmans, 1948), pp. 14-17.

[2] Quoted in John Lukacs, *Historical Consciousness: The Remembered Past* (New Brunswick & London: Transaction Publishers, 2009), p. 18. For a lively account of the rise of historical consciousness, connected with European revolutionary tradition, see Edmund Wilson, *To the Finland Station: A Study in the Writing and Acting of History* (New York: Doubleday Anchor, 1953).

Discerning God's presence and intentions in history is much easier done regarding biblical times than post-biblical times, for the simple reason that God explains the events in the Scriptures, whereas outside of them we only have patterns either very generally predicted or discernible by human wisdom. So, for example, we know from direct revelation that the events of the exodus were orchestrated by the Lord as a judgment on Egypt and for the liberation of Israel. We know that the tragic events leading up to the exile of Israel into Babylon were caused by the unfaithfulness of God's people resulting in God's displeasure. The central event in redemptive history is the death and resurrection of Jesus Christ. It is no wonder that Jesus' birth, ministry, speeches, and the events at Calvary are particularly well attested (there are no fewer than four Gospel accounts of them). So are the first decades of the Christian church, especially in the book of Acts, but also in various letters and in the book of Revelation. We needed to get those right, so the Lord kindly accommodated.

However, matters are less obvious in the centuries after these pivotal events, since we have not been given the road map. Two opposite errors can be made.

The first is known as 'providentialism.' This is the view that says we may know with a good degree of certainty when and where God is operating in history. Let me give an example which might be amusing in retrospect, but was anything but humorous at the time. At the beginning of the American Civil War, both sides more or less believed in God's providence and claimed him for their causes.

The South had seceded from the Union, believing that the North was interfering with its way of life, including the practice of chattel slavery. The Rev. William Harrison of Knoxville, Tennessee, declared that Jesus and his disciples were Southerners, and that Judas was a Northerner. The liberal theologian James Warley Miles wrote to a friend, 'It would be impiety to doubt our triumph, because we are working out a great thought of God—namely the higher Development of Humanity in its capacity for Constitutional Liberty.'[1] As could be expected, when things did not go well for the South, more sober notes were sounded. For example, three years into the war, the Rev. S. H. Higgins told the Georgia General Assembly (Georgia being a Southern state) that, 'while God intervenes in history to effect his own ends, his intervention does not necessarily signify his favour.'[2]

The opposite error is to say we simply can never know what forces are at work in the intrigues of history. Here, the claim is, 'the secret things belong to the LORD our God,' and so pretty much everything outside of special revelation by the prophets or in the Bible is kept secret from us (Deut. 29:29). But if that were true we could never make sense of historical events. While we cannot know for sure where God judges, where he blesses, where and how he intervenes in human affairs, still, we can know something about his

---

[1] Quoted in Eugene Genovese, *A Consuming Fire: The Fall of the Confederacy in the Mind of the White Christian South* (Athens & London: University of Georgia Press, 1998), pp. 37-38.

[2] Eugene Genovese, *A Consuming Fire*, p. 39.

dealings with humanity, and we may make educated historical judgments. It doesn't have to be guess work. Two principles may guide us.

The first is the number of predictions that are given to us in the Scriptures by which we may examine historical trends. The first and foremost is that there will be conflict between the forces of evil and the forces of good, culminating in the victory of Jesus Christ (Gen. 3:5; 1 Tim. 2:15; Rom. 1:20; Rev. 20:1-3, 10). We are warned that this is a process, and that though Jesus inaugurated the victory, we do not yet see everything in subjection to the victor (Heb. 2:8).

Jesus gives us a number of clues about how history will run its course until the end. He tells us the wheat and the weeds will grow together in the present era, and will only be separated at the end (Matt. 13:24-30). This should warn us against making premature judgments about winners and losers. Other Scriptures tell us to identify believers and distinguish them from unbelievers. Their profession of faith, the consistency of their life, and other factors help us make decisions about who belongs to the church and who does not (Matt. 18:15-20; 2 Cor. 2:5-11; 2 John 6-11). Such decisions will never be flawless on this side of the final judgment, but they may come close. Jesus broadly outlined the main features of history between his first and second comings. A number of these are predicted in his so-called Olivet discourse (Matt. 24:1-51; Mark 13:1-37; Luke 21:5-36). The temple will be destroyed; many will falsely claim to be the Messiah; 'nation will rise against nation and kingdom against kingdom'; there will be earthquakes and famines;

persecutions will abound; the gospel of the kingdom will be proclaimed throughout the whole world.

The second principle is that the historian's craft must wisely combine careful attention to the events and trends to be measured, with a sense of what is right and wrong, and where the gospel is at play in those events and trends. The history of world missions would seem a fairly straightforward area for the discernment of God's hand. From the beginning at Jerusalem, spreading to Samaria and to the far ends of the earth, the spread of the gospel has had a remarkable effect. Historians can identify not only the countries and the numbers of converts, but other turning points which have affected the spread of the gospel of the kingdom. Historian Mark Noll has described twelve turning points which gave special impetus to the growth of the church in the world.[1] They include the fall of Jerusalem, the Council of Nicaea, Benedict's rule, the schism between East and West, the Diet of Worms, and the Edinburgh Missionary Conference. Each of these shows how historical circumstances, guided by providence, help shape the decisive places in which the effective spread of the gospel was launched.

What about events less seemingly tied to biblical themes? While always being willing to handle the data with great humility, still, the historian should be able to identify certain trends. To pick one issue out of thousands, what

---

[1] Mark A. Noll, *Turning Points: Decisive Moments in the History of Christianity* (Grand Rapids: Baker Books; Leicester: IVP, 1997).

can we say about World War II? Here, we may assert a few certainties. Hitler's fanatic racism had to be stopped. The West had a general sense that its civilization was at stake, and thus the allies felt compelled to go to war against the barbaric extremes of the Nazis. They did so using the criteria of just war, which had been carefully developed by the church through the centuries, and was still embedded in people's consciences, whether or not they knew the theological tradition.

Then, on to less certain territory. Where was the church in Germany? In the rest of Europe? Why was not more done for the Jews? And what is the responsibility of the major stakeholders in the aftermath of the war? Where are we now, after the end of the Cold War? What should the posture of the Christian church be? Perhaps the Christian mind has a good deal of homework to do before it puts forward answers to some of those questions. And that is a lesson in itself. We do not have all of the answers to such questions. But we do have a number of remarkable commentators who can give us portions of what we need.[1] The point here, though, is that the Christian mind has the responsibility, and the privilege, like the children of Issachar, of discerning the times in order to inform God's people how to live (1 Chron. 12:32).

[1] It is impossible to cite them all here. Two scholars have inspired me, but they only tell a part of the story. Os Guinness, *Renaissance: The Power of the Gospel However Dark the Times* (Downers Grove: Inter-Varsity Press, 2014); and Niall Ferguson, *The War of the World: Twentieth-Century Conflict and the Descent of the West* (London: Penguin, 2006).

Culture and the Arts

Finally, a brief word on other voices within the moral order. Though many Christians stay away from various aspects of culture and the arts, they impoverish themselves by doing so. To be sure, some Christians have been conversant with the arts. Perhaps the art form most familiar to them is the verbal. They read literature and are inspired by a good poem or a well-told story. From the great classics to modern fiction, the best literature bristles with insights. More than just a storyline or a memorable character, an author's ability to craft words is exquisite in itself. When destined for the stage, such words may come with great power. Even if you are not a theatre-goer, you are likely to be familiar with a good many texts by Shakespeare or Thomas Stoppard. Is there weak literature? Of course. The Christian mind will need to be educated into recognizing good writing and indifferent writing, or even cheap writing.

Music has also been of particular value for most people. Martin Luther once declared, 'Next to the word of God, the noble art of music is the greatest treasure in the world.'[1] Setting texts to music has double impact. It may be Scripture, or it may be other texts, such as *Lieder* (song) or arias, but these make for great inspiration. Music articulates meaning even when there are no words as clues. Of course, there are many styles and many uses for music, and the Christian mind will have to learn to discern which are

[1] From Foreword to Georg Rhau's Collection, 'Symphoniae iucundae,' in *Luther's Works*, Vol. LIII, *Liturgy and Hymns*, ed. Ulrich S. Leupold (Philadelphia: Fortress Press, 1965), p. 323.

more edifying and which are less so. Summary judgments are often pronounced before the time is taken properly to examine various styles. Too often, we hear, 'I know what I like,' rather than, 'I enjoy what is good.'

Less familiar to many Christians are the visual arts. Some do have acquaintance with the great painters in the Western canon, from Leonardo to Rembrandt to Monet. They feel much less at home with contemporary visual art. They might even wonder what some of the objects displayed in museums have to do with art. Yet modern art can repay close study. Clearly, the visual arts today are no longer in the great Renaissance tradition where biblical or mythological figures were immediately recognizable and were depicted in order to instruct us in some virtue. And yet, surprisingly perhaps, there is an irrepressible religious meaning in much modern art. With our Christian mind, what should we be looking for?

Adrienne Dengerink Chaplin tells us, counter-intuitively, that the arts ought to give us heightened experience and understanding of the world through our senses. She contrasts this approach to one that says the arts should lift us up or help us leave off mundane experience, which is more Platonic than Christian.[1] She pleads for an 'embodied experience of our environment.' Chaplin believes that only when we are tethered to physicality can we then allow our imaginations to soar. Many modern artists are exploring

[1] Some of Dr Chaplin's thoughts are collected in *Comment*, a review accessible both in print and on line. See https://www.cardus.ca/contributors/adchaplin/.

embodiment that has a higher meaning. Christians should welcome their efforts, while at the same time be wary of their hazardous man-centredness. One example is Cornelia Parker, who mounts installations and invites us to meditate on their implications. One such construction is called *Cold Dark Matter: An Exploded View*, shown at the Frith Street Gallery in London.[1] She explains in the subtitle that it consists of a garden shed and its contents blown up. The work invites you to think about explosion, a subject she has depicted often. The message? Our world is fragile, where quietness is suddenly disturbed. Rather than being repulsed by what is not familiar, we should 'test everything; hold fast to what is good,' while also abstaining from evil (1 Thess. 5:21).

Whatever the realm, from science to history to the arts, the Christian mind will look for ways in which human beings manifest their being made after God's image. They possess an inescapable sense of deity. Even if they are busy running away from God, they can only do so in a God-haunted manner. Art historian Hans Rookmaaker once said he could preach the gospel more convincingly in an art gallery than on a street corner. The point was not to disparage street preaching but to encourage us to look at the arts as vivid illustrations of our humanity and the need for God's grace. The same can be said in all of the disciplines.

[1] 1991. See http://www.frithstreetgallery.com/shows/works/cold_dark_matter_an_exploded_view.

For Further Reading

Where to Start

John R. W. Stott, *Your Mind Matters: The Place of the Mind in the Christian Life* (Inter-Varsity Press, 1972)

Harry Blamires, *The Christian Mind: How Should a Christian Think?* (Servant Publications, 1980)

K. Scott Oliphint, *Know Why You Believe* (Zondervan, 2017)

William Edgar, *Reasons of the Heart: Recovering Christian Persuasion* (P & R Publishing, 2003)

In More Detail

Herman Bavinck, *Reformed Dogmatics, Vol. II, God and Creation*, tr. John Vriend (Baker Academic, 2004)

Cornelius Van Til, *The Defense of the Faith*, 4th edition, ed. K. Scott Oliphint (P & R Publishing, 2008)

Martin Luther, *The Freedom of a Christian*, tr. Mark D. Tranvik (Fortress Press, 2008)

John Frame, *Doctrine of the Knowledge of God* (P & R Publishing, 1987)

Irving M. Copi, with Carl Cohen & Kenneth D. McMahon, *Introduction to Logic*, 14th edition (Routledge, 2016)

Vern S. Poythress, *Logic: A God-Centered Approach to the Foundation of Western Thought* (Crossway, 2013)

Alvin Plantinga, *Warranted Christian Belief* (Oxford University, 2000)

The Bigger Picture

David F. Wells, *No Place for Truth: Or Whatever Happened to Evangelical Theology?* (Eerdmans, 1993)

John Murray, *Principles of Conduct* (Eerdmans, 1957)

J. I. Packer, *Knowing God* (Inter-Varsity Press, 1973)

Robert Wuthnow, *The God Problem: Expressing Faith and Being Reasonable* (University of California Press, 2012)

Herman Bavinck, *Reformed Dogmatics*, Vols I-II, tr. John Vriend (Baker Academic, 2004)

Banner Mini-Guides

The Bible: God's Inerrant Word
Derek W. H. Thomas

The Christian Mind: Escaping Futility
William Edgar

The Church: Glorious Body, Radiant Bride
Mark G. Johnston

Growing in Grace: Becoming More Like Jesus
Jonathan Master

Regeneration: Made New by the Spirit of God
David B. McWilliams

Salvation: Full and Free in Christ
Ian Hamilton

Sanctification: Transformed Life
David Campbell